Dedication:

To the living, loving pulse of Mother Earth
and all of her sacred children.

To Asheyana and Josh.
Thank you for your wonderful research
and for sharing your own true nature
so beautifully in the world.

Contents

CHIP RICHARDS

The Secret Language of ANIMALS
Oracle Cards

BLUE ANGEL® PUBLISHING

THE SECRET LANGUAGE OF ANIMALS

Published by Blue Angel Publishing®
80 Glen Tower Drive, Glen Waverley,
Victoria, Australia 3150
E-mail: info@blueangelonline.com
Website: www.blueangelonline.com

Guidebook and card messages by Chip Richards
Card artwork by Jimmy Manton
Artworks Copyright ©Blue Angel Gallery Pty. Ltd.
Edited by Tanya Graham
Designed in Paris for Blue Angel Publishing®

Blue Angel is a registered trademark of Blue Angel Gallery Pty. Ltd.

ISBN: 978-1-922161-08-6

Introduction

"I love to think of nature as an unlimited broadcasting station, through which God speaks to us every hour, if we only will tune in."
– George Washington Carver

There was a time when our ways were intimately woven with the pulse of the natural world. The answers to life's great questions were sought not in books and on websites but in quiet communion with the voices of Mother Earth. From the mighty whale to the tiny bee, each animal and element was embraced as sacred family – honored for the gift they bring to the greater circle of life. When eagle took flight, she spoke to our vision. When snake crossed our path she called for discernment. When the wind shifted direction or the light changed, it clarified our thoughts and feelings for the journey ahead.

If each animal and element reflects a different aspect of our own true nature, what happens if we lose one of these sacred species from existence? Do we lose also their unique gift to our world?

Since I was a child, I have always felt a deep sense of connection with the natural world. From my childhood in the mountains of Colorado, through to my adult life on the coast of Australia, I can honestly say that almost all of my most profound experiences, realizations, creative inspirations and awakenings have occurred within (or directly following) moments of communion with nature. In recent years, extended time in the wild with whales and dolphins, time in the field running with horses and time in the forest connecting with birds, trees and bees have all deepened my sense of reverence for the gifts and the pulse of Mother Earth. Amidst the rapid pace of our modern world, it takes something for us to step off the racetrack and entrain with this pulse. But she is waiting there every moment. A simple step of bare feet into the grass, a momentary dive into the water or one pure breath drawn from deep within is all that is needed to remember and return to our true sense of home and connection to life.

I believe that each animal and element holds an essential key and qualities vital not only to the ecosystem they live in, but to the greater balance of all of life. If we were to lose the animal, we would risk losing the special quality that they bring to the world. With this in mind, I felt deeply called to create this work to serve as a vehicle to share the unique and essential voices of some of our planet's most endangered species. For truly, what would life be like without the qualities of mastery and resonance of the great Blue Whale? Or the power and loyalty of Lion? What would we do without the spontaneity and vibrancy of Fairy-Wren? Or the honor and empathy of Elephant? May we never find out!

When I first started researching, I was overwhelmed by how many thousands of animals and plants are threatened, endangered or on the brink of extinction. So much so that the simple act of "choosing" made it almost impossible to begin this work. The animals and elements within this deck are no more special or important than the others, they are simply the ones that spoke to me first. They are a very small representation of the endangered voices in our world today, but their messages and gifts are beyond measure. In connecting with these, I have been lead to many others with essential and miraculous messages to share.

When Blue Angel Publishing asked me if I would be interested in creating this work, *The Secret Language of Animals*, I felt truly honored. The overwhelming feeling that I had while writing has been humility at the incredibly complex yet profoundly simple perfection of each animal and element's unique gifts and role in the greater web of life. In this spirit, I welcome you to the Secret Language of Animals, and I honor you for the unique and essential part you came to play in this great creation song.

The Secret Language of Animals is a doorway to reconnect with the wisdom of nature through the messages of a handful of our planet's most threatened species. By honoring the insight they bring to us, we deepen our connection to our own path and calling.

The only real "secret" is that many of us have forgotten that these incredible allies are sharing their gifts with us in every breath of every day. All that is required of us is to take time to enter the natural world, open our senses... and be. My greatest intention is that this work not only ignites your connection with the "essence" of these sacred animals, but that it propels you to venture into direct connection with the animals and elements themselves. For, the messages contained within this guidebook are just a glimpse of what waits for you beyond the pages, within the pulse of Mother Nature. May these cards be an invitation to awaken the next level your connection with your own true nature in all aspects of life.

Listen to the whispered call of the Secret Language of Animals... what message or gift is waiting to be awoken in you?

See you out there in the field of all possibility!

With peace, passion and deep gratitude,
Chip Richards

A man's moral worth is not measured by what his religious beliefs are, but rather by what emotional impulses he has received from nature during his lifetime.
– Albert Einstein

My profession is to always find God in nature.
– Henry David Thoreau

Using the Cards

We each have our own unique ways of communicating with the Universe – giving and receiving messages and gifts from God, Nature and our Higher Self. The way I connect with these cards varies from day to day. Our human ways often like to overcomplicate things, but animals are incredible teachers of simplicity. In this light, I often find that the message of one animal is quite enough to absorb and connect with for a day (or several days!). And yet there are also times which call for more expanded reflection. The following are just a few suggestions that you may wish to explore as you begin to discover your own unique and natural way along the path of connecting with the Secret Language of Animals.

MESSAGE FOR THIS MOMENT – SINGLE CARD READING

As part of a morning practice to begin your day, it can be quite empowering to simply shuffle the deck and wait until one card presents itself or calls out to your hand to pick. You can spread the deck before you or simply shuffle in your hands until you feel to stop. Before you read, take time to sit quietly with the card and connect with the image and energy of the animal itself. Listen quietly to the inner voice that may already be waiting to reveal a message to you. Listen to the elements and call of nature around you. When you are ready, read the words and find what part of the message speaks most powerfully to your heart today.

It may be the entire message or it may be just a few select phrases or a single word. Feel what resonates most for you, sense what actions may be called for, and when you are ready, thank the animal spirit for speaking to you and step out into your day with an openness to continuing this dialogue with the natural world that you have just begun.

Note: As a slightly expanded variation of the single card reading, sometimes when a card emerges from the middle of the deck, I also take the top and bottom card from the deck and include them as supporting energies to the first card drawn.

ELEMENTAL SPREAD

The Secret Language of Animals deck is divided into five primary elements – Water, Earth, Air, Fire & Wood – each with eight animals and a special 'Element card' – plus an overall Gaia card that is inclusive of all. The Element cards can be likened to the Major Arcana cards of a traditional tarot deck. If an Element card is chosen within your spread, this brings an over-arching theme or energy to the rest of the cards in your spread. Each elemental card is inclusive of all the animals within that element. One way to explore the specific Elements in depth is to separate the Element Cards from the rest of the deck and choose blindly among the five. Once a single element is chosen, take time over the coming days to choose among the animals listed under that element to deepen your sense of focused connection to that Element and its gifts for your path.

MEDICINE WHEEL SPREAD

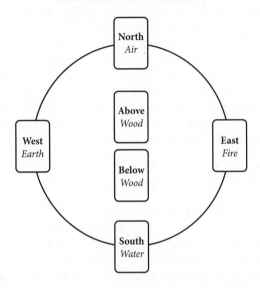

A powerful way to explore the combined energy of Animals and Elements is to create a spread in the shape of a sacred Medicine Wheel, with a chosen card in each of the four primary directions (North, South, East and West) and 2 cards in the center (Above and Below). The card at the top of the wheel is symbolic of the North, the energy of your mind and the Element of Air. The space to the left of center is symbolic of the West, the energy of your physical body and the Element of Earth. The space at the bottom of the circle is symbolic of the South, the energy of your emotional body and the Element of Water. The space to the right of center is symbolic of the East, the energy of your spirit and the Element of Fire. Within this deck, the center of the circle is symbolic of your place in the greater cycle of life, captured in the Element of Wood – the sacred Tree of Life. For this, you will need a further two cards, representing 'Above' and 'Below' and the balance of Yin and Yang (to be place in the centre of the spread).

Each card in the spread brings a special message to a different aspect of your being. You may wish to choose cards from the entire deck to fill each of these spots or narrow your focus to select within the animals of each specific element for each area of the wheel. Trust your intuition, for many animals have messages that travel well beyond their selected element.

TOTEM VISION

Totem Animal and Elemental connection is an honored tradition held by many native people around the world. Our Totem Animals are more than momentary messengers. They are ongoing allies, partners and guides in our journey through life. Different native traditions have various ways of discovering the animals and elements that "live in their heart". Some are handed down by tradition through the tribe, some are revealed in vision quest and many are discovered through real life experiences with animals and elements themselves. During times of deep reflection and visioning, *The Secret Language of Animals* deck can be used as a doorway to help reveal your own Animal Totem connection, using any of the above methods (or one that you feel guided to create on your own). I find the Medicine Wheel Spread to be particularly powerful in creating a full picture of my place on the path of life and the great energy of support, connection and guidance within it.

As with all of the messages and gifts of this book, the above are offered not as end-points but as doorways to discover your own journey. In my experience, the most profound Animal wisdom and Totem connection almost always comes from our direct communion with the Animals and Elements themselves. May this deck be an invitation to immerse yourself in the wonders of the natural world... and a reminder of the sacred union you share with all beings in the great circle of life.

Card
Messages

WATER

"We call upon the waters that rim the earth,
horizon-to-horizon,
that flow in our rivers and streams,
that fall upon our gardens and fields;
And we ask that they teach us and show us the way."

- Chinook Indian Blessing

WATER
Feeling, Awakening, Expression, Life

1. WATER
Feeling, Awakening, Expression, Life

Water is the life blood of our planet. The rhythm keeper, the valley forger, the carrier of energy and sustenance. Born from the cooling steam of ancient volcanic fires, water covers over 70% of the surface of the globe and fills nearly 70% of our bodies. We are water beings living on a water planet.

From tiny ice crystals on mountain peaks down to the silent center of our deepest oceans, water is the holder, the guardian and giver of life. From storm clouds and waterfalls, to the gentle trickles of fresh springs that bubble up from deep within the Mother – water cleanses, renews and connects. Water flows through obstacles, removes barriers, breaks down mountains and awakens life. As a supreme channel of sound and vibration, the water of our planet carries the migration songs of whales and honors the whispered prayers of all who bring their message to its shores.

Used by many cultures to honor ceremony and rites of passage, water reveals to us the secrets of life's cycles and brings us into contact with the rhythm of our own sacred journey home.

THE MESSAGE
Amidst the rapid pace of modern life, we can easily be overrun by the roles, responsibilities and agendas of the mind. We may find ourselves struggling to forge a path, feeling thirsty for meaning and fulfillment, without realizing there is a clear river of natural

expression running right along side us... an ocean of possibilities before us... and an infinite wellspring within us, waiting to guide our way.

Water now enters your life with an invitation to surrender your worldly burdens and open your heart to the creative power of your emotions and the higher currents within. As the rain drop finds its way through sky and trees to join the tiny mountain stream that will one day deliver it back to the sea, water guides your steps from quiet visions to the full manifestation of your dreams. Not with strain and force, but with natural, empowered flow, guided by a deep inner compass calling you home to your true Self.

If you feel stuck, confused or unsure what actions to take, bring your questions to the Water. Observe Water's graceful power and natural, effortless way. Let it be your teacher and a clear reflection of the infinite possibilities now available to you. This is a time of great creative possibility. Water honors your journey and welcomes you into its depths. Celebrate this moment as a blessing – a rite of passage opening the way to a fresh wave of flow-filled expression. Come to the water. Share your prayers, intentions and gratitude with the element of Water.

I am one with the ocean of life. I flow with the river of all possibility and I sing my songs with the tides. Divine water, move through my body and bring the gift of life to my whole being!

BLUE WHALE
Unity, Resonance, Magnificence, Mastery

2. BLUE WHALE
Unity, Resonance, Magnificence, Mastery

Whales have lived in peace on Earth for 50 million years. They are integral to the biological balance of the planet, and they provide a golden model for intuitive wisdom, community and communication. Their peaceful ways and willingness to connect with humanity despite the lack of mutual respect they often receive, reveals a level of mastery and benevolence aspired to by our greatest earthly teachers.

At over 100 feet (30m) long and 200 tons in weight, the Blue Whale is the most immense and physically powerful creature on the planet… yet it is also among the most gentle and mysterious. We catch glimpses of this incredible being only when it surfaces to breathe, but know very little of its deep journeys and great migrations in between. Its song is the loudest of any animal noise... and yet it comes at a frequency that cannot even be heard by humans. It is thought by scientists that the whale song, unimpeded by landmass, could circle the globe and return to its sender. Whales often travel in small numbers across vast distances, but their song keeps them ever in close communion with each other, weaving a web of sonic resonance through the waters of our planet.

In the lore of many Native people, the whale symbolizes the beginning, the creation of all life. Birth and rebirth. Many cultures still see whales as divine beings. If the body of a dead whale or dolphin is washed ashore in Ghana or Vietnam, its finder must mourn the death like a brother and bury the body in ceremony.

THE MESSAGE

There is something immensely powerful about being in the presence of Whales. If you have ever been on a boat when a whale surfaces to breach or breathe you will have felt a sense of wonder reflected in the eyes of all who witness the moment. Many people say their entire lives have been changed by a single moment of eye contact with these great beings of the sea. Why is this? Perhaps because whales, in their immensity and grace, give us a glimpse at a much deeper and vaster aspect of our own being. They awaken in us a consciousness that has been here as long as they have. They remind us of the song of our own soul that is woven into the great creation song of life. They call us to return to our deep connection with beauty, harmony and balance. They remind us who we really are.

The great Blue Whale brings this message to you now. You are a vast and masterful being. Your presence in the world brings a great gift to the song of creation. There is no need to prove or defend yourself against anyone or anything. You need only stay focused on the pure and simple expression of your light in the way that you live, breathe and share your gifts with the world. With the same wonder that you see the whale, the whale also sees you. Your soul is deeper than the ocean. You are safe to swim in these waters. Allow yourself to dive down deep, past the surface waves of the mind, through the emotional undercurrents to the vast stillness at your very center. The great whale spirit welcomes you here and shares with you a song of pure peace and conscious mastery. This is your song. Accept it. Embrace it. Live it. Be it.

I am one with my divine purpose. Conscious, aware and connected to all of life. From the still center of my being, my thoughts and actions bring peace and balance to the world.

POLAR BEAR
Solitude, Friendship, Strength, Resilience

3. POLAR BEAR
Solitude, Friendship, Strength, Resilience

Polar Bear is the ancient wisdom keeper of the North. Intelligent and fearless. Native tribes have long honored the Polar Bear as a great ally and bridge to the spirit world. His white coloring reflects his purity. His strength amidst adversity is a gift to all who wish to journey past their own fears and limitations to the open space beyond.

Weighing up to 1600lbs (730kg) and standing up to ten feet tall, Polar Bears are incredibly strong, resilient and more adaptable than other members of the bear family. As one of earth's largest carnivores, they move at great speeds on both ice and land and can swim up to 100 miles (160km) without stopping to rest.

Existing in the frozen extremes of the water realm, Polar Bears embody water's full spectrum of emotional power. They are masters of preserving energy and strength for the hunt, and yet they have also been known to lose their temper, throwing ice and kicking piles of snow in disappointment when they miss their prey in a chase. They are deeply solitary animals traveling long distances alone, and yet amidst the dark hours of winter they are known to often form lasting friendships with other bears, arctic foxes and even tamed huskies in the wild.

Perhaps because of their extended periods of solitary travel, when a group of Polar Bears comes together, it is known not as a flock, herd or pride, but as a 'celebration'.

THE MESSAGE

Amidst the pressures and extremes of daily life, sometimes we can lose sight of where we are going. Polar Bear brings you the gift of inner strength and the ability to move with great power and intelligence beyond what may have limited you in the past, into the full experience of that which calls you now. Step forward with confidence and determination. Polar Bear brings the gift of resilience driven by a purity of spirit that focuses not on the obstacles but on the higher vision of the ultimate outcome you are seeking.

Polar Bear says to speak your truth and find constructive ways to express the emotions that rise within you. His message is to hold strong to what you know, while remaining flexible and open to what emerges. Find the balance between the extremes by walking your journey long enough to let that which no longer serves you fall away and melt back into the sea.

Sometimes your growth calls for solitude and quiet introspection. Sometimes your heart yearns to come together in communion with another. Sometimes you must conserve your energy and sometimes you must leap with full, unbridled expression in the pursuit of your dreams. Wherever you find yourself presently, Polar Bear comes as an ally, guiding you to the heart center of your own inner strength. Take time to walk with Polar Bear, measure your approach and gather your energy close. When the moment comes to move toward your goal, you will do so with absolute clarity and power.

I am anchored in my center and aligned with my purpose.
When I am still, I am quiet within. When I move, I move with
great power. I am purity in motion, endurance in the night.
I am inner strength and wisdom in full expression of my light.

4. DOLPHIN

Joy, Light, Flow, Compassion

Mammal cousin to the great whale, Dolphin has been revered throughout the ages for its grace, intelligence and lightness of being. With ancient beginnings as a creature of the land, Dolphin evolved over time to master a life between worlds, breathing air and giving birth as we do, but from the quiet sanctuary of the Water realm.

In ancient Greece, Dolphin was honored as a messenger of the gods. To kill a Dolphin was a crime punishable by death. The Celts saw the Dolphin as the protector of sacred wells and holy water and Sumerians linked Dolphin to Ea-Oannes, the deity of the sea. In Egypt, Dolphin was an expression of the goddess of Isis, while Christian symbolism depicts the Dolphin as an aspect of Christ. Indigenous Australians have long revered dolphin as a great guardian spirit, from which some of their tribes are direct descendants. Regardless of origin, countless tales throughout the ages tell of dolphins reaching out and interacting with humans in friendly, protective and playful ways.

Considered the "king of fish" by many ancient cultures, Dolphin brings to us the energies of compassion, community and playful generosity. Traveling in close-knit family pods, Dolphin moves like light in motion, leaving a trail of grace, magic and joy for all to share.

THE MESSAGE

Weaving the elements of water and air, of sun and moon, of yin and yang... Dolphin brings to you the gift of freedom found in playfulness... power expressed through harmony... and uniqueness found in connection – to yourself, your community and that which makes you come alive. When life becomes too serious and bound by effort and goals, Dolphin reminds us of the energy of spontaneous flow. Dolphin now calls you into the realm of synchronicity with trust in the magic of the moment. The time is now to follow the energy of inspiration on your path.

Dolphins are one of the only creatures that truly value joy and pleasure, both as an end result and a way of being. The message of Dolphin is simple but profound: if you want to feel happy with the outcome of your endeavors, seek first to enjoy the journey. If you want to love what you are doing, start by giving yourself permission to do more of what you love. Dolphin is here to remind you of the magic of your dreams and of visions you once held, but thought you had lost. It matters not what waves may have passed you by. Now is a fresh moment and dolphin is calling you to surf the magic of your inner call.

Be open to new friendships and be ready to share your gifts graciously with others. They are needed in the world. As Dolphin harnesses the power of waves to soar with great speed and lightness of being, now is a time to follow the energy of that which excites you. The waves of life are your playground. Let your inspiration carry you!

*I follow my bliss, knowing that I am worthy to experience joy.
Riding the waves of inspiration within me, I bring great joy and
light into the world.*

5. SALMON
Faith, Determination, Independence, Change

Born in the rock pools of mountain streams, Salmon's journey is that of the hero. A great circle of transformation, venturing from its fresh water origins into the wide open ocean, where it must learn to live, breathe, grow and survive before one day answering the deep inner call to return again. Following the inner compass of its ancient heritage, Salmon embarks upon an epic quest against the current, defying waterfalls and predators before returning to the exact same stream bed of its beginning. There it spawns, giving rise to a new generation before completing its journey and dissolving back into the stony river bottom from which it came.

In many cultures, fish are deeply symbolic of the gifts of transformation, fertility, abundance, determination, good fortune and creative flow. Salmon embodies and expresses all of these attributes in the bold adventure and archetypal cycle of its life. Thought by Celtic Druids to be the oldest and wisest of all creatures, Salmon represents the full spectrum of the Shaman's quest for knowledge and the journey to discover the essence of our own true Self.

THE MESSAGE
Sometimes we think we want our reward to be handed to us on a platter, but the truth is that most of life's great gifts are made

sweeter by the journey we go on to reach them. Great challenge and seemingly impossible odds reveal to us that we are great beings, far more capable than we realized. Without the currents and waterfalls, Salmon would have no way of discovering its own ability to rise above and find the way through. When Salmon swims into your world it honors you as the hero of your own life journey. Salmon calls you to recognize your greatest challenge as your greatest opportunity to discover and experience strength, resourcefulness and capabilities within you that you would otherwise never know existed.

The message of Salmon is to be willing to stand on your own, to walk a different path to others when your heart calls you to do so. Follow your instincts and creative impulses, even when it takes you down a slightly different path than others may be going, or expect you to. Your energy and enthusiasm will quickly gather the support of others, but if you find yourself venturing solo into unchartered waters, know that this too is part of your journey. Each must find its own way through. But clarity is power and when your movements are driven by a deep inner call, the river of life will reveal pockets of flow and secret passages within the currents to support your journey, even when the surface waves seem to be rising up against you.

While Salmon appears to be fighting against the current, in truth its passage is supported by a series of reverse undercurrents flowing in the direction of its journey home. Seek allies and pockets of energy that support the direction you wish to go. As with Salmon's shift from fresh water to salt and back again, change and transformation is part of your journey. When the moment calls, don't be afraid to change direction, or let go of a previous aspect of your being in order to open the way for your next chapter of expression.

Salmon reminds us that though we may travel far away, we

are each native to somewhere. Honor the ancient heritage of your own culture. Your returning is part of the hero's journey – to share gifts that you have gathered and to nourish yourself in the waters of your origins.

As the hero of my own life story,
I answer the quiet call of my spirit.
Change is my friend. Clarity is my power.
My life is a great adventure, always guiding me home.

DUGONG
Trust, Grace, Mystery, Humor

6. DUGONG

Trust, Grace, Mystery, Humor

Dugongs, like dolphins and whales, are mammals who, long ago, adapted their form for life in the ocean. But unlike their Cetacean counterparts, Dugong's vegetarian grazing habits and gentle, slow-moving ways reflect a stronger link to their ancient days on land. Growing to lengths of ten feet long, Dugong looks similar to the walrus and has a fluked tail resembling that of a whale, but strangely its DNA links it more closely to the elephant.

Referred to as the 'Beauty of the Sea' in Egypt, 'Queen of the Sea' in Kenya and 'Princess Dugong' in Indonesia, Dugong's story brings the great mystery of feminine power into the emotional currents of the Water realm. Thought to be the source of mermaid legends, early sailors caught glimpses of Dugongs swimming near the surface waters and believed them to be half-human, half-fish creatures, singing to their lonely spirits in the night.

Though 'herds' of several hundred Dugongs have been known to gather and journey together, Dugong spends most of its time grazing quietly alone or in pairs. The female Dugong lives for up to 70 years and only mates a few times in her life, spending two or more years in companionship and caring for her children.

THE MESSAGE
As an ancient bridge between the realms of land and sea, Dugong honors the woven wisdom of your physical body and your heart.

For Dugong, the key to survival is not to fight or flee, not to chase or hunt, but to move with grace and ease, calling and allowing that which is needed to come to you.

Dugong's message is to slow down, breathe deep and take time to be. With Dugong, more is achieved through less effort. Allow the feminine power within you to sing its song into the waters, summoning that which you require and desire most. Action may still be required, but first find your place in the moment with an aim of 'doing' from a higher state of 'being'.

With Dugong, no matter how busy you seem to be, know that there is always time to do what is most important. Take time to honor those you love. Celebrate the gift of children and embrace your role in nurturing the spirit of those younger than you on the path. Rush nowhere and you will find yourself everywhere you need to be just at the perfect time. Start by being right here... now.

I am present. I am calm. I trust the abundant flow of life that now brings to me all that I need and desire. With peace and gratitude, I share my gifts with others.

7. SEA TURTLE

Beginnings, Self-reliance, Journey, Home

Turtle is one of Earth's great grandfathers, evolving into form more than 200 million years ago, before mammals, birds, snakes and even lizards. At home on land and in the water, Turtle's patient way and steady, gentle strength enables it to outlive most other animals (including humans), with a life span often reaching 100 years or more.

But Turtle's journey does not have an easy beginning. For water turtles such as the great Leatherback, when the tiny soft-shelled beings break from their egg in a hidden nest of sand, they and hundreds of their brothers and sisters must race for the water's edge to escape the pursuit of birds, lizards and other predators. For those who reach the water, the journey to safety and survival has only just begun. It is thought that as few as 1 in 1000 sea turtles make it to their first birthday, but most of those who do, remain for many years to come, carrying the torch of their species. Most soar within the weightless realms of water for up to 25 years before returning to the same area once again to mate (and for the females) bring their great bodies back onto land for the first time since birth and begin laying eggs of their own.

Nomad of the ocean realm, one of Turtle's great gifts is its shell, a home he is born with and can never be separated from. It's an intricate weaving of 60 different bones connected together.

Most turtle shells are divided into 13 sections, honored by many indigenous cultures to symbolize the thirteen phases of the moon each year.

THE MESSAGE

The message of Turtle is to simply begin. Great journeys are made with small steps and steady progress. Turtle wisdom recognizes that our first steps into any adventure and endeavor may feel clumsy, dangerous and scary. But when the moment comes to birth an idea, start a new friendship or take your first steps down a path that calls your heart, there is no substitute for simply answering the call. Begin. Follow the energy of the sun. Steady progress feels good. You need not hurry, but don't wait until the conditions are perfect. The act of beginning makes the conditions perfect.

In the same way that a giant, 1700-pound Sea Turtle soars weightlessly in the sea of his belonging, you will find a sense of buoyancy rising within as you give yourself the gift of immersing in the energy of your calling. No matter how great the task may seem before you, no matter how tiny your first steps may appear, know that you are honored for that which you bring to the circle. You are part of a bigger story unfolding, and your dreams are connected to many others.

Turtle teaches us endurance through peace, patience and gentle perseverance. Turtle calls you to find a sense of home within your own being now and to know that your journey through the world will always be supported.

I am home within myself and in the world.
I trust the call of my great spirit.
When it comes, I hear it and I begin.

8. CRAYFISH

Protection, Perseverance,
Vulnerability, Regeneration

Freshwater cousin to the Lobster, armored one of the water realm, Crayfish brings to us the gift of polarity – opposites that complement each other. Strength and vulnerability... independence and interconnectivity... protectiveness and receptivity... These are the ways of the Cray.

Born into eggs, called "instars", Crayfish spend their lives journeying the depths of underwater landscapes. With an external skeleton that surrounds a soft inner body, Crayfish has no bones at all. They are fiercely protective against those who oppose them (and will literally tear each other's limbs off in a fight) but they are gentle and loving with their mates (and their limbs grow back!). Crayfish walk forward (journeying many miles across the underwater landscape, holding claws with each other for support) but swim backwards (much faster than their walk!).

When Crayfish molt each year, they shed their entire outer shell, then eat that shell to retain the calcium and phosphates it contains. In their vulnerability they go into hiding until the new shell hardens around their body. As bottom dwellers, Crayfish are living filters for the water, but they are also highly sensitive to contamination. The presence of healthy Crayfish in a body of water is a sign that the water they are living in is also healthy.

THE MESSAGE

When Crayfish crawls into your world, he calls you to consider your current life structures. The gift of structure provides safety and stability as we move and grow in the world. There are times when certainty and firm support are needed to harvest the strength for your steps on the path. But Crayfish comes to remind you that yours is also a path of transformation and becoming. Within this journey there will be times when you need to break free from the current form in order to expand into a higher way. This does not mean rejecting or abandoning your current circumstance, but rather (as Crayfish does each time it sheds, then eats its shell) to harvest the lessons and gifts of what has been in order to evolve and grow into a form that will fully honor and support who you are now becoming.

Sometimes when we feel boxed in by our circumstance, our first response is to contract, pull away, push back or defend. What would happen if instead of contracting, you expanded your vision to take in a much bigger picture? What would happen if instead of pulling away to avoid conflict with another, you stepped in closer with a commitment to working together? What would happen if instead of pushing back or defending your point of view, you opened yourself to truly see the world through the other person's eyes, seeking a solution that honors both and all.

When we think we need to be more "realistic", sometimes what we really need is to be more inspired. Crayfish calls you to expand your perception of the possible, rather than shrinking to fit the current form. Challenge yourself to see beyond what you or others may have thought possible yesterday and create a whole new form of expression that honors your greatest gifts and who you truly came here to be.

You may feel called to spend time in quiet solitude in order to cultivate your inner strength and allow your new self to integrate.

Know that this is normal, in fact it is an essential part of your journey. Know too that within your vulnerability there is great power. When it comes time to share yourself with others, do so authentically, from your heart and you will open the path to new levels of connection and depth of expression together.

Harvesting the lessons of all that has been...
Honoring the gifts of all that is
I expand my way of seeing, being and doing in the world
For the good of all.

SHARK
Perception, Focus, Fear, Action

9. SHARK

Perception, Focus, Fear, Action

Ancient guardian of the Water realm, Shark has swum the waters of our planet for over 400 million years. Before the time of dinosaurs, before Turtle wisdom first entered the sea, before Whales sung their first migration song and way before you and me... there was Shark.

For many, Shark evokes only feelings of fear, but a closer look reveals a complex being of great sensitivity and unique paradox. Shark is one of the most sensitively in-tune creatures in the ocean. Considered by scientists to be the 'nose of the sea', Shark has a highly attuned sense of smell, can feel the vibration of other animals' movements hundreds of feet away, can hear sounds from thousands of feet away and knows the exact direction from which the sound is coming. Shark exerts great strength and power yet has not one single bone in its body (her entire body is made of cartilage). The Whale Shark is the biggest fish in the world with over 4000 teeth, and yet feeds only on microscopic plants and animals. For as long as Shark has guarded the ocean realms, it has never evolved a "swim bladder" so it must remain in constant motion to allow oxygen to move through its gills. Without perpetual movement forward, Shark would sink and die.

Within many ancient cultures, Shark represents the power and authority of Nature, the mastery of emotions and the rite of passage from one phase of life into another. Shark is clear, resourceful and intimately connected with the cycles of life. Those who meet Shark with respect, deeply value the gifts she brings.

THE MESSAGE

Shark is a threshold guardian. Her role is to test your commitment to the path you have chosen. Not with intention to thwart or swallow you in the process, but to give you the gift of experiencing yourself moving beyond that which may have held you back in the past. When Shark swims into your waters, she does so not to invoke fear, but to give you the opportunity to face your fears or hidden concerns and allow them to dissolve into the clear waters before you.

Shark connects us with the creative element of water, with a level of discernment that allows us to be clear, decisive and direct. Use your sensitivity to inform your actions. Harness the power of your emotions, but do not be consumed by them. Be willing to be dynamic and bold, to act on opportunities as they arise, but without clinging to the outcome you think you need. Shark's message is to stay in motion and focus on that which moves you forward, while remaining open to other gifts that may emerge on the path.

Shark brings to you the power of heightened sensitivity. Take time to be alone. To find your quiet center and tune into your physical senses. These are your gateways to the subtle messages in the world around you. Listen, smell, feel and see what Shark senses and you will gain great insight into your experience. Know that she is with you, honoring your steps into the unknown and offering great protection for your journey into it!

I am clear, decisive and aligned.
Deeply in tune with my senses,
I move with confidence, grace and power.
My fear is a doorway to my higher path.

EARTH

"The Earth does not belong to man;
Man belongs to the Earth. This we know.
All things are connected like the blood which unites one family.
Whatever befalls the Earth befalls the sons of the Earth. Man
did not weave the web of life,
he is merely a strand in it.
Whatever he does to the web, he does to himself."

– Chief Seattle

10. EARTH
Physical body, Grounding, Nurture, Cultivate

Our planet is 4.5 billion years old. Seventy percent of her surface is covered by water, but this water, in all of its forms is cradled by the ancient valleys, canyons and basins of Earth. Soil, stone, sand and clay... minerals, metals and crystals. Each emerging first as magma from the molten furnace deep within Earth's core, hardening into rock, breaking down into sediments and finer forms before eventually returning to the very core where it began.

To Native people of many nations, Earth is the healer, provider of nourishment and material sustenance. As the element of stability, fertility, beginnings and endings, Earth is the keeper of home and family. To many, Earth is the manifestation of divine vision in physical form.

Until the modern era of city streets and synthetic shoes, our connection to Earth's healing, immune-boosting and hormone-balancing electromagnetic field was guaranteed through daily direct contact with her soil and sands. It comes as no surprise that modern science has discovered measurable benefits from taking time each day to be "grounded" or "earthed".

THE MESSAGE
Step outside. Take your shoes off. Stand there. BE. The element of Earth embraces you with a message to find stillness within

motion. To be grounded in order to reach far. To settle into yourself in order to find freedom.

Earth brings the gift of realness and tangibility. The Earth path is simple, direct, complete. Whole. There is no need to strain, force or hurry. But your consistent, committed presence is required. Don't get lost in the big picture or swallowed by the details. Just concentrate on being where you are right now. Show up. Be present. Follow through. Focus on the simple things that need to be done and you will feel a sense of great accomplishment. Now is a time for building, cultivating, anchoring yourself into steady committed action to provide a solid foundation for that which is ready to come through you. A great new chapter or phase of your work in the world is ready to unfold and now is the time to ground it in. Earth it! It's not so much about ascending into lofty planes, but rather bringing the energy of infinite possibilities into physical form. The earth element may call for physical work, but you will find great fulfillment in taking committed action toward your ideas.

If you have come to a cross roads or decision that must be made, connecting with the element of Earth will help you know what is needed next. Take time to sit, stand or walk barefoot in the grass, sand or soil. Feel the pulse of the Earth align with your own and from this place, reflect on your path. Allow your body to tune into each option. Which direction are you being pulled? There is so much that can be solved by simply going outside and connecting with the element of Earth. Work the soil of your life, plant the seeds you wish to grow and tend your garden with simple devotion and grounded action. In days to come, your harvest will be great and shared with many.

I am One with the element of Earth.
Grounded. Connected. Empowered in my Being.
My actions are real and committed,
Aligned with the energy of my highest dreaming.

LION
Power, Loyalty, Leadership, Family

11. LION
Power, Loyalty, Leadership, Family

From the gods of ancient Greece to the goddesses of Egypt, from Hinduism to Buddhism, family crests and coat of arms, Lion has long been embraced as a symbol of strength, courage and dignity. Sacred protector of thrones, palaces and shrines, Lion is the guardian of our quest to live our highest values in life. In the ancient art of alchemy, Lion symbolizes the purified attributes of gold.

With a roar that can be heard up to five miles away, a running speed of 50 miles per hour (80km/h) and an ability to leap as far as 36 feet (11m) in one bound, Lion embodies the essence of physical prowess. Lord of cats and king of the animal kingdom, there is one special difference between Lion and virtually every other member of the cat species – Family. While most cats live a solitary existence, Lion's path is one of belonging, teamwork and togetherness. Deeply affectionate in rest and highly coordinated in action, each brings unique strengths to play a vital role in the journey of the "Pride". Though they spend 16-20 hours each day resting, when Lion moves, the world knows about it.

THE MESSAGE
When Lion comes to you he comes with a call to awaken a power within that is your birthright. Not through struggle, forcefulness or contrived effort but through the simple expression of your true Self, ignited deep within. When Lion roars he does so not

to gain approval, but to boldly claim his place in the world. I AM here. Lion is now calling you to make such a stand. There is nothing you need to learn or gain from the outside world to be fully who you are. The time is now for you to embrace your unique strengths and allow them to lead you to discover your greater place within the whole.

If you feel stuck or less than empowered, bring yourself into the open fields or quiet shores where you can be alone. Take time to reconnect with the truth of your inner fire and let yourself roar. Awaken the power lying dormant within. Feel it rise from the earth into your heart and body. You are a great and noble being. Your leadership is now needed to take your 'pride', team or project to the next level. Do not shy away from your power, but allow yourself to breathe deeply and accept that you came here to fully express your gifts in the world. What is your heart calling you to do? Lion is leadership and abundance. Lion is loyalty to the calling of our heart. Speak your truth. Embody your strengths. Honor your gifts and the gifts of others within the balance of work and pleasure. Solitude and togetherness. Be the Lion you are.

I breathe into my centre and awaken my power.
Aligned with my tribe, I am the full expression of my
unique purpose.

12. MOUNTAIN GORILLA

Reverence, Contemplation,
Community, Inner calm

Once thought to be fierce and aggressive, Gorilla brings the gift of immense physical strength (about 20 times that of humans) through gentle reflection, grace in motion and mutual respect.

As our closest kin in the animal kingdom, Gorillas share 98% of our DNA, and their peaceful way of being reveals many of our most aspired attributes. They are highly intelligent and cooperative, inherently affectionate, considerate and inclusive of each other. They form close bonds with those who live in their troop, and they share responsibility to care for both the young and the elders of their tribe. They never seek conflict and yet they are courageous and valiant in their commitment to protect their family from danger. In power struggles with each other, Gorillas may raise their voice, beat their chest and even shake trees to assert themselves, but rarely will they use physical force against each other to maintain peace and balance in the group.

Shy and nomadic by nature, Mountain Gorillas make a fresh bed every evening from the branches, leaves and grasses of their surroundings. As vegetarians, they serve the biodiversity of their environment by spreading the seeds of fruit and plants they eat throughout the forest.

THE MESSAGE

When Gorilla comes into your world, she comes with the gift of reflection and deep inner calm, born from the knowledge that you are strong beyond measure and wonderfully supported in this world. Amidst the rapid pace, pressures and expectations of our modern life, Gorilla calls you into the sanctity of your own magnificence, reminding you that you can create your own world based on values of peace, trust, community and quiet abundance. Honor the spirit of youth, both within you and around you. Be also respectful of your elders. Seek their wisdom and guidance as a doorway to the ancient knowing that dwells within your own being.

No matter what may be going on around you, Gorilla comes as a reminder that we always have the ability to take the higher ground – to observe with great understanding, to demonstrate deep inner strength in how we stand and speak and move. Do not back down from challenge, but there is no need to chase it either. You are stronger than you know. Speak clearly and honestly from your centre. Lead with a calm knowing and thoughtful consideration, seeking always the path that will serve all. Take time to share the simple magic of life with those you love.

There is no need to rush ahead. Move with quiet grace and the path will rise to meet you, providing abundantly for all of your needs. Create comfort wherever you are by taking time for simple rituals and self-care activities that put you in touch with the deep peace of your heart centre. Where is your private sanctuary? Go there, and find yourself within it.

I breathe deep into the sanctuary within me.
I am grounded. I am strong. I am whole and complete.

SNOW LEOPARD
Mystery, Agility, Belief, Sensitivity

13. SNOW LEOPARD
Mystery, Agility, Belief, Sensitivity

Perched in a snow-covered tree, silently aware of life around her, snow leopard peers through pale green eyes, watchful, stealth and full of mystery.

Home to barren regions of mountain, snow and rock, Snow Leopard is lighter than most big cats. But with widespread paws for wading across snowfields and a thick furry tail that is nearly as long as her body – used for balance and to shield her mouth and nose from harsh winter winds – Snow Leopard is well equipped for her surroundings. While her territory is spread across a vast area of Central Asia, her shy, nocturnal ways means she is almost never seen in the open.

While other big cats are known for their fierceness and danger posed to humans, Snow Leopard walks a path of silent harmony and non-aggression. Unless her own cubs are being threatened, Snow Leopard will often choose to back off and let other predators finish a well-earned meal simply to avoid conflict. Preferring the quiet sanctity of her independence, she journeys alone much of the year, coming together only at mating time with others of her kind. Thriving in places where most would not venture, Snow Leopard is a Lunar animal, pure of spirit.

THE MESSAGE
When Snow Leopard moves into your world, she brings a sense of quiet belief and purity of motion. Patient and deeply sensitive,

Snow Leopard teaches us the art of agility – balancing stillness and observation with dynamic action, informed by the silent mystery of our intuition.

Snow Leopard asks you to looks beyond the surface to the spiritual teachings and gifts in your surroundings and experience.

Snow Leopard says it's okay to walk your own path and to find comfort and serenity in your own company. Seek quiet solitude and in that solitude you will regenerate your being and heighten your connection to your own sense of direction. Tread quietly on the path that calls, not to impress others, but simply because it feels right to you. Snow Leopard calls you to walk your path with a vision that sees through shadow and darkness to the pure possibility beyond. There are times to be outwardly expressive of your gifts and there are times to quietly harvest your energy and keenly observe the world around you, so that when you act, you do so with great speed and agility. Take time to get in touch with your own whispered guidance and inner truth. In the mystery of Snow Leopard, one moment the way may appear blocked, but in the next quiet breath a doorway opens where once there was none. Be patient and ever present to the subtle signs of the moment. Smile deeply and be ready to leap when the moment calls. There is magic and mystery all around you.

I am present to the great possibilities around and within me.
When I move, I move in harmony
with the pure magic of life.

14. CARIBOU

Perseverance, Resourcefulness, Movement, Determination

White wind blows across the arctic field sending ancient whispers into the forest. The lead stag raises his head, sensing the moment for his herd to move. Something distant stirs him into motion. He moves... and the rest follow. While many hibernate and huddle close, Caribou run, and run together. Under his guidance and leadership all are included.

Honored among Laplanders as a source of sacred partnership and sustenance, Caribou is revered for its wisdom, creativity and inventiveness. Few are equipped to survive the harsh conditions of the far north like Caribou. Hollow, insulated fur to shed freezing water... a strong snout capable of digging through snow to reach food... broad, concave hooves that tread across deep snow...two separate stomachs to store food, and two separate circulation systems to conserve heat in its body during winter. Both male and female Caribou grow antlers, revealing that all can be warriors. And both shed them during the cold winter months to carry less weight.

Feeding on aged moss and lichen from the ancient forest floor, Caribou are connected to the deep history and sacred lore of the ground they walk and all who have come before them. Their movement honors the seasons and the changing needs of the greater herd. When two male Caribou fight to win the rights to lead the herd, the greatest danger they pose to each other is their own determination that would have their antlers lock together leaving both unable to eat.

THE MESSAGE

There is a season for all things: a time to be alone, a time to come together, a time for stillness, a time for movement and committed action. The richness of life is found in the balance and Caribou brings this gift. Caribou's message is to trust the cycle of your own seasons, honoring the full expression of who you are. When it is time to rest, give yourself the gift of true self-care and rejuvenation. Nurture yourself until your cup is full and naturally flowing over. When it is time to move, let your actions rise from a deep inner calling. Move with great trust and commitment, knowing that you will reach your goal. You are capable of far more than you realize.

Caribou brings great strength, resourcefulness and resilience to your path. Know that you have within you all that you need to move through whatever apparent obstacles may rise to meet you. The path may not unfold exactly as you imagined it, but with each challenge embraced comes the discovery of new gifts, resources and aspects of yourself that you would otherwise not have known you have. Once awoken, these gifts are yours to keep and share for all seasons to come. This is the gift of Caribou – to activate the hidden gifts and infinite resources available to you by embracing the path that calls for their full expression.

Caribou balances time in quiet solitude and time of great collaboration with the herd. Now may be a time for you to step up as a leader and to powerfully include others in your journey. Caribou's gift is to lead by example – inspire others into action by moving into inspired action yourself. The only obstacle that could get in your way is locking horns with others... Stand your ground, but walk in peace and seek always to embrace the higher path that honors all. Life is movement. Embrace the seasons of your soul.

In stillness and movement
In silence and expression
In solitude and togetherness
I honor the seasons of my soul.

15. WHITE RHINOCEROS

Stability, Confidence, Steadiness, Abundance

Red dusty plain. Shrubs and desert trees. Dry air, warm earth... warm, steady breath. Grey lashes blink slowly over dark eyes, reflecting strength and confidence. Second largest land mammal next to elephant, Rhino's armored presence and five-foot horn gives him an air of aggression, but in truth he is a passive, peaceful grazer, roaming open spaces in the quiet of his own company. White Rhino are the calmest and most sociable of all living species of Rhinoceros. Living in small groups, they communicate with a wide variety of grunts, growls, snorts, squeaks and bellows. They have highly sensitive hearing, a keen sense of smell and an ability to run 30 miles per hour (about 50km/h) with great agility, but much prefer wandering the savannah in quiet seclusion and wallowing in cool mud-baths to protect their sensitive skin from sunburn and insect bites. As a vision of confidence, steadiness and grounded abundance, Rhino appears to be happy to spend most of his days alone, and yet shares a unique, symbiotic relationship with oxpeckers, who feed themselves on ticks from the Rhino's body and return the favor by screeching out whenever danger is near.

THE MESSAGE

When Rhino enters your world he comes with a message to

breathe deep into your centre and quietly remember who you are – a deeply magnificent being, way more powerful than you may even realize. Take time to stand in the sun and plant your feet in the soil. Feel your connection to all things. Allow your outer protective layers to relax, knowing they will be there to protect you if you need them. But now is the time to trust your strength to be yourself and stand with quiet confidence in the world. Rhino's gift is to remind you that while life sometimes calls for moments of decisive and powerful action, our greatest strength is often found in the presence that we exude simply by owning our gifts and knowing who we are. The key to avoiding power struggles with others is to first come to peace with the power residing deep within.

Spend time in contemplative solitude. Find comfort and sanctity in your own company. Worry not about ascending to the high planes... now is the time to draw upon the grounded energy and abundance of the earth. To nurture yourself with the simple pleasures of life and the elements of earth, sun and water. Find your version of Rhino's mud bath and give yourself the gift of full replenishment. When you merge back into the world, seek first to spend time with those who honor you most and celebrate your unique contribution. Communicate your needs to your close allies and be conscious about respecting the often unspoken needs of others. Be open to unexpected partnerships with those whose gifts complement your own. When creative relationships flow, each brings a special part to the whole and all are made stronger as a result.

I am here to express myself powerfully in the world
I honor my gifts and the gifts of others
I stand strong and move with quiet confidence
My greatest power is the natural expression of who I am.

16. ELEPHANT

Honor, Empathy, Responsibility, Cooperation

A wave of floodwaters rush through a native village, leaving destruction and chaos in its wake. Hours before the event, a group of Elephants pull their chains up from the ground and trumpet people to the safety of a hilltop. Hours later, these same Elephants wade through the rubble, retrieving children and struggling survivors... bringing order back to the village. Highly sensitive and socially connected, Elephants have much to teach us about the power of community and the gift of cooperation. Largest of the land mammals, they share a similar gift of altruism, intelligence and gentle power as their oceanic counterparts, the whale. To the Chinese, Elephant brings happiness, longevity and good luck. To the Hindu, Elephant is vibrantly expressed as Ganesha, the god of good fortune, protection and blessing upon all new projects.

Elephants have one of the most closely-knit and loyal societies in the animal kingdom. They communicate across great distances through low frequency sounds beyond human perception (much like whales) and through an ancient language shared in the vibrations of their stomping feet. They live together for 60-80 years and females only ever leave the herd when they die. During the female pregnancy, which lasts for 22 months, she selects several "babysitters" to help care for her and her young one when it arrives.

In an Elephant herd, if one of the members becomes sick, others will bring it food and protect it until it is healthy again. If it dies, the herd becomes very quiet, grieving their loss. They will dig a shallow grave and cover the elder with dirt and branches. Even herds that come across the remains of an unknown Elephant, will pause at the grave to show respect. There are many stories of Elephants developing deep friendships with other animals, rescuing each other, other species and humans from danger. With the largest brain of all land animals, Elephants have a highly developed sense of self, spatial awareness and emotional maturity. They commonly share profound levels of humor, compassion, cooperation, creativity, playfulness and companionship with others.

THE MESSAGE

When Elephant enters your life, she brings blessings of the highest order. Through the path of gentle power and cooperation, she calls forth the gifts of compassion, community and higher purpose. Amidst the rapid pace and pressures of life, sometimes we become disconnected from the deeper emotional needs of ourselves and others. As we race to complete our to-do list, we lose contact with that higher sense of Being that inspires our most meaningful actions in the world. Elephant trumpets a clear reminder that you are a great force for good, here to serve the higher path of humanity by embodying the higher values of your own divine nature. The time is now to trust your higher purpose and find powerful ways to live with an open heart in the world. As you learn to recognize, embrace and accept your Self, you will awaken a sense of freedom that allows you to transcend imaginary barriers between yourself and others, empowering you to live in ways that serve the highest good of all.

Reclaim a sense of community in your life. Honor the magic

of children and the deep wisdom of your elders. Draw together those who are closest to you. Call on them to support you in the gifts you are now birthing. There is a great energy of support all around you, you may just need to ask. When your cup is full and you realize just how blessed you are, you will begin to see opportunities to share that energy with others. You will be a source of good and a blessing on other people's journeys. You will bring support and assistance when they least expect it. Now is a time for patient power and gentle strength. Embrace your emotions and the full spectrum of your being – from joy and playfulness to sadness and deep reflection. Each has a part to play in your rich journey of awakening the divine blessing you are.

I see the world through an open heart
My thoughts, words and actions
open the hearts of others.

17. PYTHON

Discernment, Detachment,
Transformation, Renewal

On the edge of an old-growth rainforest, as birds and animals come and go, seeking, hunting, chasing, fleeing... one lies quietly waiting. Coiled around the smooth skin of a native tree, Python allows the dapple sun, the warm rain and all that she needs to come to her in perfect time.

Oldest and largest of the snake family, Pythons have tiny spurs on their body reminiscent of where their ancestors may have once had legs. In their current form, they swim, climb and they grow up to 30 feet (9m) in length and weigh over 310 pounds (140kg). With a highly tuned sense of smell and heat sensing organs in their lips, they are able to maneuver silently through the dark, and can remain totally still for many hours camouflaged by the environment before striking suddenly at passing prey. Shedding its skin regularly as it grows, Python retreats into the shadow worlds of quiet isolation during winter months to call back its energy.

To the ancients, snake represented both goddess and god, as well as the shadow side of spirit. In India, snake is the symbol for the Kundalini energy, coiling around the spine as life force, birth, death and renewal. Some Native American tribes revere snake as the masculine symbol of protection and assertive power, while others honor it for the feminine energy of mothering, creation and the moon. Celts saw the snake as a symbol of secret knowledge – the protector and guide between what has been and what will be.

THE MESSAGE

Python silently enters your world to open the way to deep transformation and renewal. She calls forth the full realization of your dreams, not through exerted effort and chasing but through quiet mastery of one of your greatest creative powers – intention. Take time to listen closely to the ancient calling of your soul. Clarify what you really want and allow this vision to ignite a fire of new possibility within you.

Nothing renews our spirit more powerfully than the awakening of a dream. Bold visions dissolve past perceptions of the possible, and awaken within you a whole new way of being. Resist the temptation to rush off, sharing this new dream with others or wasting your energy chasing after it. Take time instead to allow the embers of your desire to grow inside, harvesting the energy of your vision... calling it closer to you. With Python's ancient knowing finely attuned to the rhythms of life, she will help you sense when it is time to act and to do so with great, assertive power and accuracy. She can assist you to be patient and calm, but to seize the moment with great power when it matters most.

Maintain focus, but don't let your idea of how you think things are supposed to happen, stop you from seeing what emerges before you. Letting go of your attachment to both past and future outcomes will give you an ability to feel the pulse of highest possibility and follow the energy of the moment. Be willing to look into the shadows. To see beyond the surface of your circumstance into the deeper truth and higher gifts this moment brings to you.

I release the past to awaken the new.
I see my world through the eyes of who I am becoming.

LIZARD (TUATARA)
Dreaming, Sight, Knowledge, Hidden gifts

18. LIZARD (TUATARA)
Dreaming, Sight, Knowledge, Hidden gifts

Native to New Zealand, Tuatara is the last surviving species of an ancient order of reptiles that lived along with dinosaurs 225 million years ago. Referred to as primitive and thought by many to be a living fossil, in truth Tuatara's pace of evolution is more advanced than any other animal – which is why it has survived for so long.

Tuatara takes up to 35 years to reach maturity and can live beyond 100. They change color, can drop their tail when under threat, and shed both their spine and skin as they grow. Adult Tuataras can go for an hour without breathing allowing them to be totally still and silent, blending in to the ancient rocky outcrops of their homeland. They are cold-blooded but unlike most of the lizard family, prefer cooler weather to hot.

Tuatara is born with a third eye with its own lens, cornea and retina on the top of its head, thought to give it heightened sensitivity to time of day and season. While this third eye is eventually covered over with scales, the two remaining have the ability to focus and turn independently. Each eye also has three eyelids (closing from the top, the bottom and from the side), one of which is translucent so it can be closed without impeding Tuatara's vision.

They share the burrowed homes of seabirds (who fly during the day when Tuatara sleeps, and nest at night, while Tuatara hunts), recalling a distant age and realm when lizard and bird may have shared one body... as dragon.

THE MESSAGE

Sometimes, as we journey through our normal busy lives, a whisper comes to call us from a place deep within. At first it may be subtle – so quiet in fact, that it could be easily missed among life's other pressures. But if we pause to listen we will hear it like the distant rumble of a thundercloud within. This is the calling of our ancient inner knowing, summoning us onto our path.

Tuatara speaks to the ancient call of your spirit. Now is the time to awaken your dormant abilities and choose the path that honors the full expression of your unique gifts. The role you came here to play was decided long ago. A specific energy was greatly needed and you chose to bring it. Listen to the part of you that is not bound by daily tasks, but is alight with the mission of fulfilling your deeper contracts with life.

Sometimes making choices means giving up certain activities in order to make room for the greater dream to come through. Even if choosing one path requires letting go of another, know that there is no risk of losing yourself. When you make a true commitment to the one, you naturally include the all. Tuatara says, bask in the warmth of your ancient knowing. Embrace your power to see all possibility and to choose the path that truly honors your soul. In doing so, you honor the soul of the world and all of life.

There is no need to rush ahead, but when you connect with your own sense of inner knowing, when you claim your deepest gift, you will know that you have no choice but to move forward into your unique calling in the world.

I am one with the ancient knowing of my soul
I feel its calling in my body, I live its truth on my path

AIR

---

*"Jonathan Livingston Seagull . . . was no ordinary bird.
Most gulls don't botherto learn more than the simplest facts of
flight – how to get from shore to foodand back again.
For most gulls, it is not flying that matters, but eating.
For this gull, though, it was not eating that mattered,
but flight. More than anything else, Jonathan Livingston
Seagull loved to fly."*

– Richard Bach, *Jonathan Livingston Seagull*

***

*"Forget not that the earth delights to feel your bare feet and the
winds long to play with your hair."*

– Khalil Gibran

19. AIR
Thought, Alignment, Breath, Intention

Air is everywhere. Subtle, invisible, yet intimately woven into every step of our journey. Our first breath marks our life's beginning and our last honors our passing to the other side. In between, our personal exchange with Air is constant (about 26,000 breaths a day!) and impacts the function of our body, our state of mind and virtually every aspect of our being.

To the Inuit of the north, the Air Spirit is a kind and beneficial spirit who controls the rhythms of the seas, skies and wind. To the Aztecs of Mexico, the wind-god puffs the sun and moon into motion. To the Chinese, Air is the purified essence of Qi (life force). In India we find Prāna, the sacred breath of life. To Native Americans, Wind is a great living force that has always whispered secret messages and guidance to those with open hearts and ears to hear. All beings are intimately connected with the energy of Air.

One powerful way that Air reveals itself is through its influence on other elements. In the Water realm, Air currents create waves on the ocean's surface that travel and build for thousands of miles before rising to a great climax and breaking on the shore. To Fire, Air is the lifeline of every flame... with equal power to expand and extinguish. On Earth, Air carries seeds, scents, bird songs and mating calls. Air builds and destroys dunes, chisels canyons and allows light beams and spider webs to cross vast spaces to reach their destination. In the Wood realm, Air makes music as it moves through trees, pollinating and exchanging vital plant essences and allowing the lungs of our planet to breathe. The Latin word for 'breath', spirare, has given rise to words such as aspire, inspire, perspire and spirit - all of which speak to the essence of this great gift to our world.

THE MESSAGE

Have you ever had the experience of concentrating on something so intensely that you forgot to breathe? Eventually your body reaches its limit and you realize (consciously or unconsciously) that in all of your focus to achieve, you have been denying yourself a fundamental element needed to reach your aim. In an instant, you draw a breath, and with it comes a wave of renewed energy and life force to inspire your endeavor.

Air comes to you now with an invitation to open yourself to receive such a wave of energy and inspiration in your life – by taking conscious responsibility for your thoughts as the creative architecture of your world. Air calls you into the realm of the mind, with the reminder that thinking is much like breathing. We do it constantly, but often automatically, reactively, with very little conscious attention to how it is impacting our experience. When we bring our attention to our breath, we ignite a positive source of energy that ripples through our entire being. When we consciously choose our thoughts, we awaken an invisible power to transform our world.

If you are not happy with what you are seeing, then look first to the thoughts and silent meditations that may be contributing to this outcome. Before you run around trying to change what the outside looks like, take time to choose thoughts that will support your true desire. Call upon the element of Air and, through your breath, you will awaken new visions and perspective to guide your steps. We are always creating something with our thoughts. What do you choose to create today? What will you breathe into being? Find a quiet place where the Air is fresh and clean... Open yourself to the sacred whispers and messages in the wind as it shares its message with you today. With clarity comes great power.

Spirit of Air! Purify my thoughts and intentions
To inspire the pathway of my highest visions.
I am One with the breath of life.

EAGLE
Vision, Freedom, Authority, Inspiration

20. EAGLE
Vision, Freedom, Authority,
Inspiration

Great sky keeper. Bridger of Heaven and Earth. Vision maker for the new dawn. Native American lore tells the legend of the Thunderbird, a mighty winged one, whose eyes shot forth with piercing bolts of lightning and whose massive beating wings summoned rain into the sky.

Standing three feet tall in the body with a seven-foot wingspan and eyesight up to seven times more powerful than our own, Eagle flies higher than any other bird and embodies the essence of the great Thunderbird even today.

To many First Nation people, such as the Aztecs, Mayans, and Pueblo Indians, Eagle symbolized the rising sun. Known as a Sacred Messenger from Heaven and the "Eye of the Sun", Eagle brings the gift of expanded perception and celestial power – carrying prayers to the Creator and returning with a vision for the path ahead. The Celts also honored Eagle as an ally to Water, with her unique ability to see into the depths with great clarity from above.

When being courted by a prospective life partner, the female Eagle flies up with an object (such as a stick) in her talons and drops it, watching to see if her male suitor will be committed and fast enough to dive down and catch it before it lands. She knows this daring feat may need to be repeated live with her offspring one day, should they falter in their first steps from the nest. If the courtship is successful, they will mate in similar fashion, mid-dive between Heaven and Earth. Seen by many as the chief of all winged ones, Eagle's daily habits share a deep connection with each of the elements of Air, Water, Earth, Fire and Wood.

THE MESSAGE

When Eagle soars into your skies she brings with her the gift of freedom born of the courage to see beyond all limits. Eagle comes to awaken the visionary in you. She calls you to the high place of your purest dreaming. She comes to remind you that you did not come here to be tangled or suppressed by life. You did not come here to be weighed down by the details of your day-to-day, but to rise with the breath of your great spirit, to stretch your heart and vision beyond what may have once seemed realistic or appropriate – into the wide open field of all possibility.

Eagle medicine brings the power to build a bridge between your greatest aspiration and your current reality. Eagle knows there is a time to perch, a time to study from afar, a time to soar above and a time to dive with great focus toward that which you are seeking. As you prepare to embark upon a new life change or creative endeavor, take time first to bring yourself to higher ground. Breathe in the mountain breezes that give birth to lofty visions. With Eagle's view, you will see with great clarity not only the field of infinite possibilities before you, but also what actions are needed to realize your vision. And with this clarity comes the energy and inspiration to claim all that is your dreaming... and more. Move with Eagle's power and grace, and you will find that great heights can be reached with ease, while maintaining a grounded connection to the earth.

From the mountain top of my being
I see a world of infinite possibility
I open my wings, and let go of limits
My Great Spirit lifts me higher.
I bring visions of Heaven back to Earth.

21. FALCON

Focus, Action, Purpose, Aspiration

Hovering quietly in the thermal breeze, the winged warrior focuses on movement in the sky below. Black eyes open wide with purpose as long, pointed wings propel him into a dive of great intensity. His focus remains until he gains the object of his desire, mid-flight.

The Peregrine Falcon is the fastest animal in the world. With a diving speed of close to 250 miles per hour (400km/h), it can reach up to 150 miles per hour (250km/h) in normal flight when chasing prey.

In early Egyptian hieroglyphs, Falcon was the symbolic word for "god". The Egyptian god Horus was a Peregrine Falcon, and many of the sky deities (including the sun god Ra) had Falcon heads. In some cases, the human soul was pictured with a human head and Falcon body. In the afterlife, Falcon was the healer of souls and an escort back to the world of souls. When a king passed from this life, his ascension was known as the "Flight of the Falcon".

Like many in the bird tribe, Falcons mate for life and breed in the same territory each year. Similar to the great Eagle, the male courts the female for about one month, often using aerial displays to win the heart of his bride.

THE MESSAGE
Falcon comes into your world with gifts of immediacy, dynamic

flight and focused action fully committed to the task at hand. With great speed and clarity, Falcon calls for you to pierce the thin veil of doubt and uncertainty that may have previously stopped you from taking bold action in the direction of your dreams. The message here is not to rush forward aimlessly, but to take time to focus clearly on the path ahead and then to take fully empowered action in the direction of our visions and our passion. It is time to do what is necessary to bring your desires and goals to fruition. The more clarity you bring to your commitment, the more complete your "Yes" is to the moment, the more you will find that obstacles evaporate in your wake and the path opens wide to greet you.

There is nothing to fear. You bring with you the energy of the sun itself. Let the dawn of the new day fill your being and clear your vision of what actions are needed in this moment. Be not limited by what may or may not have happened yesterday. Breathe deep and know that your wings are alight with divine inspiration and your greatest strength comes in motion. Take time to calculate and strategize but don't get stuck in hyper-analysis. Now is a time for action. As you move in the direction of your calling, subtle shifts in direction and focus will be easily made. Falcon calls for change of pace, shift in focus, awakening new roles and possibilities. Open your eyes to see what new opportunities, interests and passions may be hovering near you, waiting to be explored. Give thanks and seize them with full strength and power. Embrace change. Falcon calls for you to know the difference between tunnel vision and one-pointed focus.

I move with the grace of wind and the power of light
I am clarity, I am focus
I am divine purpose, in action.

22. WHITE PELICAN

Ease, Optimism, Grace, Cooperation

A wave rolls in on a misty morning from thousands of miles away. As it rises to a peak, three white figures sail along the glassy face just above the surface. Seemingly still, but gliding in dynamic motion, they sail along the rolling water like lyrics to a song. Linked in a line, closely mirroring each others' movement, they also mirror the rising rhythm of the sea itself. I Am Pelican. In the ancient art of alchemy, Pelican symbolized the legendary Philosopher's Stone – a stone that was said to turn base elements into gold. Pelican was thought to embody these same magical and transformative powers, drawing together the individual resources of a group to create the extraordinary.

A large-bodied bird with a ten-foot wing-span, Pelicans bring the gift of close cooperation and shared journeys, gliding in formation with each other to create draft and lift. Sometimes soaring in a V-shape, sometimes in a straight line just millimeters off the water's surface, Pelican share long, uninterrupted expeditions and will fly up to 100 miles (160km) a day simply to gather food in their large bills to feed their chicks.

Pelicans are known by fisherman to be finely tuned barometers, always knowing when a storm is brewing or the tides are turning. And with air sacs beneath their skin that add buoyancy, they may dive into the water for food, but they quite literally cannot sink.

THE MESSAGE

Weaving the magic of air, sea and earth, Pelican enters your world to open the way for ease, grace, cooperation and optimism on your journey. At times our thoughts and feelings can feel like opposing forces, creating stress in our body and dispersing the energy of our actions. Just as Pelican dances between the elements to create a life of gentle harmony, now is the time for you to bring together the energies of your mind, heart and body into unified motion in the world. Elevate your thoughts to gain a fresh perspective, and be willing to dive into the waters of your deep emotions to bring new understanding to the surface. As you awaken a path that honors both your higher vision and the wellspring of your feelings, challenges transform into opportunities and the waves of life become the perfect playground to soar with grace and ease.

Move through the world with a sense of congruence in yourself, and you will find your journey naturally coming into alignment with others who have discovered a similar freedom of being. The unified thoughts, feelings and actions of two or more together begin to multiply and the ocean of possibility opens wide to greet you. From the outside, your life appears like a symphony of movement that defies nature. But within your soaring ways, it is the most natural, effortless and joyful expression of who you came to be.

At ease with the alchemy of my Self.
I soar with the energy of my tribe.
Celebrated, honored, lifted by the breeze... I am flying.

ALBATROSS
Faith, Endurance, Journey, Hope

23. ALBATROSS
Faith, Endurance, Journey, Hope

I wake with a dream of a distant shore, calling me. I know not why or for how long, but I know it is calling me. I know it is further than I can see. It may even be further than I imagine it to be... and yet it calls to me. I know I must answer. I know I must begin. For deep inside I know that the voice that is calling me to that distant shore... is my own. I am Albatross.

Albatross is the largest of the flying bird family. With a wingspan of 11 feet, they spend over 80 percent of their life at sea, much of the time in flight. While their journeys call for levels of endurance that few in the animal kingdom must endure, in truth, this is what Albatross was built for. With a wing shape specially designed to travel long distances and endowed with specialized gliding techniques that minimize the need for flapping, Albatross can soar on virtually motionless wings for hours at a time. Because of this, seamen long believed that Albatross had magical powers, bringing good omens to those who cross its path in peace. Their flying technique is so efficient in fact, that they spend more energy landing and taking-off than when they are in the air.

Albatrosses breed on remote islands with large colonies of others. Males and females come together after ritual mating dances and once their bond is formed, they stay together for the rest of their lives. Over the course of their 60-year life span, their journeys will cover millions of miles.

THE MESSAGE

Albatross glides to you upon the ocean breeze, bringing renewed hope and the promise of good fortune for the path ahead. It takes courage to set out on a journey of any kind and Albatross knows that sometimes we must travel far beyond the shores of our comfort zone before we catch a glimpse of our aspired destination. When the nights are long and dark, when the wind appears to push against your passage, it can be easy to question the calling that brought you to this path in the first place. It is in these times – when our doubt is most justified – that we are called to keep our faith and courage alive and honor ourselves for the sacred nature of our journey. Albatross' message is to look beyond the wave of current circumstance and smile at the light that is emerging on the horizon.

If your current life is stretching you to reach to new horizons – inside yourself or in the world – Albatross comes to encourage you to make the leap, and trust yourself and the secret winds that guide you. There is no need to flap your wings and fight against the storm. Breathe deep instead and rise above. You were designed for this great journey. You are wiser than you know and you are honored by the spirit of the sky. There is no hurry. There is no pressure. There is no wrong way to go. Trust, with courage, your deeper calling. Embrace the vistas of the new day before you and know that your path is unfolding in just the right way. The journey will take as long as it takes and when you arrive to the distant shores of who you are becoming, you will recognize the magic perfection of each and every moment, sunrise, raindrop and breath along the way.

I trust the calling of my Spirit and soar beyond what once seemed possible. My life is a great and epic journey.
I am faith in motion.

CONDOR
Cycles, Reflection, Perspective, Release

24. CONDOR
Cycles, Reflection, Perspective, Release

Peaceful sky warrior. Sacred custodian. Keeper of the land. The California Condor soars in great circles high above the desert shrub. His discerning gaze and mighty black wings extend out from his body, catching the thermals that take him ever higher. His upward spirals are never-ending for he is one with the great circle of life.

Condor is a vulture species that was once found along the entire Pacific coast of the Americas. Along with Eagle, Condor shares the sacred title and mystical powers of the great 'Thunderbird of the Heavens' among certain native tribes of North America and the Peruvian Andes. The largest of the North American bird tribe, Condor stands over four feet from head to tail and weighs up to 18 pounds (8kg). With a wingspan of over nine feet (almost 3m), Condor soars to altitudes of 15,000 feet (4500m) and travels up to 150 miles (240km) a day in the quest for his next meal. Like others in the vulture family, Condors eat mostly carrion (dead animals) and in doing so, serve a great role in the ecosystem as part of nature's team of cleaners.

While perhaps thought by some to be dirty, Condors pride themselves on cleanliness. They bathe often, spend hours preening and smoothing their feathers and even clean themselves after eating by rubbing their heads through grass or leafy tree branches. They journey as a pairs, who mate for life, and produce only a few young over a lifetime, taking time to care for each for many months before letting it venture off on its own journey toward the sun.

THE MESSAGE

Condor circles high in silence calling you to new heights of personal awareness and deep connection to the natural cycles and rhythms of your life. As a sensitive leader tuned into the subtle currents of existence, Condor brings you the gifts of patience, perspective and vision. She offers her deep understanding of the importance of change to allow the greater picture of your life to unfold. Following nature's cycles, together you see that change is constant, and not to be feared, but rather embraced. Each piece of your story can be lovingly honored for the gift it brings before it is released back into the greater circle of creation.

Now is a powerful time for you to honor the need for quiet solitude and open yourself to the positive power of change. Take yourself to the high mountain and pray. Allow the rising thermals to clear away the energy of your daily life and give you a chance to see the greater picture unfolding before you. Examine your life from an elevated view and you will know in your heart what now needs focus for the path of your future Self... and what parts of your journey are now coming to an end. Honor each for the role it has played and be grateful for this opportunity to lovingly let it go. Open your heart to the new and allow the Universe to deliver your needs to you in unexpected ways. You need not chase or hunt. Now is a time for receiving and making the very most of what is already before and within you. What resources and opportunities are already here, ready to be honored and brought to full fruition?

Within the quiet sanctuary of my being,
I celebrate the sacred gift of life.

FAIRY-WREN
Spontaneity, Vibrancy, Support, The Muse

25. FAIRY-WREN
Spontaneity, Vibrancy, Support, The Muse

As I walk along the forest path I feel the slight energy of being watched... of being talked about... of being guided on my way. Light and friendly beings, dancing freely but with purpose. I am welcomed to the realm of the Fairy-Wren. While other members of the bird tribe bring us the perspective of great height and vision, Fairy-Wren dances into our world with the gift of spontaneous song that moves in close connection to the Earth and the subtle, shifting, magical rhythms of life.

With dome-shaped nests built close to the ground in thickets of pandanus, river reeds or cane-grass, Fairy-Wrens use the language of movement and song to communicate many different messages – from romantic courtship to danger warnings of approaching predators, to coordinated duets sung by Fairy-Wren couples to enforce the boundaries of their territory.

Celtic Bards have long been inspired by the lyrical gift of the Wren as a doorway to the Muse – that mystical source of poetry, art and song within. Beyond the spark that lights our creative fire, the Celts also honored the Wrens for their productive nature and unique way of sharing roles and responsibilities as a group to serve the greater whole. Fairy-Wrens live in extended families of 5-7 birds, with one primary breeding pair and a handful of offspring from previous years (usually males), who stay with the family to assist in raising the young of future generations, before they inherit the forest to build their own communities.

THE MESSAGE

From the deep song of your own soul, comes the spontaneous whisper of Fairy-Wren to honor the call of the Muse within and to remind you that miracles are present in all moments if our eyes are open to see and receive. Be open to change. Be open to turning completely around in fact, and back again if the moment calls. Don't be attached to one way of doing things. Sometimes when we follow an impulse or creative idea, it begins to change shape on the journey to achieving it. If we are open to the possibilities unfolding before us, we may realize that the original idea was just a doorway to another higher path. The only danger is to become so fluid that you lose site of your intention and end up flitting this way and that to chase the fleeting pulse of momentary whims. Fairy-Wren's message is to know the feeling of what you want and to move from that centre, knowing also that it may not look like you think it will. Tread lightly upon your path and be ready to see and seize moments of opportunity that you never dreamed might come your way. Think big, but don't think for too long. Trust your gut and dance with what is occurring. There is no need to fear choosing the wrong path or to become overly attached to what may have felt right yesterday. Each step leads spontaneously to the next and only when you reach the other side will you look back and see the poetry and perfection of how the path unfolds. Stay light on your feet, be open to receiving help from those who love you and be ready to spring into action, following the subtle shifts in light and energy on your path.

With deep inner strength and lightness of being
I follow my Muse and the pulse of the moment.

MASKED OWL
Insight, Wisdom, Foresight, Messenger

26. MASKED OWL
Insight, Wisdom, Foresight, Messenger

Perched in the shadows, just beyond the light, a silent figure stands motionless, almost invisible, but fully present. Observing and absorbing that which others would walk past or strain to see, Owl is the bringer of wisdom, revealer of secrets, messenger of hidden truth.

With sub-sonic hearing and vision that penetrates the night, with rapid wingbeats alternating with silent gliding flight, Owl is the "night eagle" – seeing, hearing and knowing that which others cannot. Silently she waits, watches, then moves with grace, descending upon her prey.

Because of her unique nocturnal sense and skill, Owl has often been seen as the guardian of the underworlds. In ancient Egyptian, Celtic and Hindu cultures, Owl was ruler of the night, seer of souls and sacred guide to those crossing from the physical world into the realm of spirit.

To the ancient Greeks, Owl was a close ally to Athena, goddess of wisdom and learning. To early Christians, Owl symbolized Christ's ability to illuminate our passage through darkness and challenge. Because of Owl's keen eyesight and unique ability to sense changing weather conditions, Native Americans, West Africans and Indigenous Australians embraced Owl as a keeper of wisdom, messenger of sacred knowledge and foresight. To medieval Europeans, legend held that Owls were actually priestesses and wizards in disguise.

THE MESSAGE

If Owl has swept silently into your presence, you have come to a significant place on your journey. Take this moment as a great blessing, for Owl comes with an invitation to awaken your senses to see with fearless clarity into hidden places and to experience your world in a whole new way. Great new opportunities await your experience, but they cannot be accessed by your normal worldly way of seeing. Trust your intuition but don't be limited by past perceptions. You cannot reach where this path leads by doing more of what got you here. If there is an unknown space between where you currently are and where you want to be, Owl's insight and silent wisdom will help guide your passage.

Owl calls for you to quiet your mind by slowing down your senses. Become a silent observer. Listen with your inner ear and see with eyes that look within. Remove yourself from the noise of life and come to a place of darkness, where your eyes can turn inward for a time. Give yourself a chance to breathe deeply and find peace in the shadows and silence in the inner cave of your being. Allow your fears to rise to the surface and see them for what they really are – windows to new possibility. As your eyes adjust you will come to realize that from this place of deep stillness, both shadow and light can be seen, and the power of both can be embraced, healed and woven together to fuel your higher path.

"Enlightenment" is my power to see light in unexpected places.
This begins as I discover light deeply within myself.

27. CROW

Communication, Transformation, Story, Universal Law

Ancient lore tells us that each animal spirit has a unique gateway through which they enter the sacred circle of life. Each doorway is symbolic of the gift that each is destined to bring to the world. There is a gateway for each of the animal species, through which their potential is birthed into reality. All are included... except for Crow. Crow is the gatekeeper. Crow knows the essence of all who come to the circle. He meets each at the threshold of their journey and assists their passage into becoming who they really are.

To the ancestors and Native elders, Crow is the totem of the Great Spirit, the weaver of light and dark, of inner and outer worlds. He is honored with the deepest respect. Crow's pitch-black feathers symbolize pure spiritual strength and creation. With nests perched at the top of the tallest trees, Crow has long been honored for his unique perspective and magic way of seeing and being in the world.

Each "caw" of Crow actually has a different meaning and the depth of their vocabulary gives us a glimpse at their intelligence. Crows are renowned problem-solvers, lock pickers and tool-users – they can survive in almost any situation. When one Crow solves or explores something new, others in the clan watch closely and learn... then spread the word. Crows remember the faces of those who have helped them and those who have harmed them. They not only carry this story with them throughout their life, they spread the word so that all in their clan know who to trust and who to be careful of. Celebrated by many cultures for their playful and mischievous nature, Crows form close friendships with a wide variety of animals, can be seen surfing the wind, sledding in snow and playing with sticks in the wild, and have even been known to build fake nests high in treetops to confuse predators.

THE MESSAGE

Crow is the guardian and the messenger of your unique sacred story. The keeper of Universal Law. He stands at the gateway to assist you in the transition from one chapter in life to another. From one level of being and doing in the world, to the next. As you approach, Crow calls out on your arrival, speaking the story of the steps you have taken so far, the lessons and the gifts you have gathered en route to this place. As you reach the threshold, Crow pauses and stares deep into your soul with cold metallic eyes. He asks you what you have learned and why you believe you are ready to move on to the new. What is the purpose of your path?

His "caw" is sharp and penetrating, at times intimidating. But in truth, he does this only as a game. He is not really here to test you or to hold you back, but to celebrate and herald your transition into a new realm of experience. He knows you are ready, for he has watched you every step of the way and spoken your journey into the great gatherings of the tribe. He knows who you really are... do you? Crow's penetrating stare and abrasive call is a gift, for it gives you the opportunity to strengthen your resolve and stare right back, stepping forward with even more commitment than before. As you do, Crow breaks into a smile and begins to laugh. The celebration has begun. Another hero has crossed the threshold into the realm of the possible. All smile knowing that the path ahead will rise to greet you. Welcome home.

I am a unique being
Living my story, epic and true.
I walk my own way, to my own beat
Weaving ancient wisdom into the sacred new

FIRE

---

*"In the name of the Fire, the Flame and the Light;
Praise the pure presence of fire that burns from within,
without thought of time."*

– John O'Donohue

28. FIRE

Creation, Destruction, Beginning,
Expression

It's the night of a new moon and the air
is fresh and cool. A circle of stones rests
on the earth, mirrored by an outer ring of elders and children,
gathered in peaceful reverence. All is still and silent, but for
the quiet crackling of Fire. Each brings forth a quiet prayer or
offering. Then comes music, chanting, stories and laughter, as
visions are lifted into the night sky by the spiraling breath of this
sacred light. It both calms and awakens the spirit of all who are
present.

To ancient Greek philosophers, Fire was a sign of energy and
passion. To the Celts, Fire was a source of spiritual transformation.
In traditional Chinese culture, Fire brings the masculine energy
of Yang and the power of purification. To the Aztecs, Fire is found
in the 'seven-ray sun' that symbolizes the phases of spiritual
development in the soul of man. To many native cultures, Fire
is the sacred medium through which our deepest prayers and
intentions are communicated to the Universe. With sacred herbs
offered to the embers, dreams and visions are sent to Great Spirit
within spirals of rising smoke, opening the way for manifestation
in physical form.

In nature, Fire stimulates growth, and brings renewal
and balance. At times Fire burns away and destroys the old,
cleansing and purifying the land for new growth. Different to

the downward gravitational flow of Water, Fires energy rises, moving ever upward. From the center of Earth, up through the mouths of volcanoes, Fire brings the energy of creation, giving birth to the mountains, islands and earth of tomorrow.

THE MESSAGE

When Fire comes into your world it does so with pure energy, passion and the sacred power of creativity. No matter what you feel may have held you back in the past, Fire now come to burn away limitation and awaken the full expression of your creative potential. Fire brings fresh light, forward movement, and dynamic expression... Now is the time to move!

If you are not sure which way to move or how to begin a new dream or journey, take time to sit with Fire. Light a candle or a sacred flame in a circle of stones. Bring to it your prayers, your vision and even your uncertainty. You may even like to bring an offering of sacred herbs or tobacco... Release your intentions to the higher powers of your Great Spirit within. Open yourself to receive guidance for what is now needed to create the real shifts you desire. Allow the clarity of Fire to speak to your heart and to center your being. From this place, you will step forward with clarity and confidence, with faith and power, in the direction of your dream.

We can wait all day (or life) for the conditions to be right before we begin, but in truth, it is often our beginning that calls the right conditions into being. What if you knew that the light on the path you have been waiting for is the one that is already glowing deep within YOU?

With Fire comes decisiveness, determination and the will to initiate, to ignite, to light a new spark of possibility... and follow it! Claim these gifts for your journey now. Clear the clutter and space around you to give yourself a chance to see and seize a new pulse of life force, new energy, new visions and dreams that are ready to come through you now. Get excited. Be bold and expressive. Feel the breath of God moving through you. It is time to honor the great creative being that you are by moving into courageous action. Trust the visions of your dreaming and with passion and Fire... begin.

I embrace the Fire of life within me.
Clear and centered in my purpose, ignited by creative potential
I am a force for good in the world.

WILD HORSE
Freedom, Sensitivity, Spirit, Partnership

29. WILD HORSE
Freedom, Sensitivity, Spirit, Partnership

Night wind moves through the valley, bringing the scent of a distant memory. The lead mare lifts her head, smelling the breeze. The others watch her, waiting for guidance. Her ears twitch and her hooves scuff at the earth, as she peers into the night, sensing the energy of that which comes their way. Forcing a breath through the velvet of her nostrils, she turns in the direction of their next step of freedom, knowing the others will follow. All but their stallion, who will stay behind to face any danger before joining the herd on higher ground.

Honored as a messenger of great nobility, strength, beauty and grace, Horse is woven deeply into myth and history, from Celtic lore to Christian visions, Hinduism, Greek mythology, Chinese and Native American tradition. Horse has journeyed the plains throughout the ages and shared a special bond of service, protection, transportation, victory and companionship with humanity for over 5,000 years. French naturalist, Comte de Buffon, put it well when he said, "The noblest conquest of man is to have gained the friendship of the horse."

Bestowed with the gift of clairsentience, Horse carries heightened sensitivity, deeply attuned to the energy and emotions of those around her. Horses have the largest eyes of any land animal and a memory that surpasses that of the elephant. When a domesticated horse is released into the wild it quickly sheds all traces of domestication and returns to its deeper spirit of natural freedom. "The wind of heaven is that which blows between a horse's ears." (Arabian proverb).

THE MESSAGE

Merging the freedom of Spirit with the groundedness of Earth, Horse calls you to into a woven expression of presence and power. Amidst the noise and pressures of the world around you, the message of Horse is to trust the subtle feelings of your body in order to sense what is right and true. The key to knowing what to do next is found in combining your greater vision with quiet attention to this moment right here... and here... and here. Each step holds the potential for both simple connection and glorious miracles. Horse medicine helps you weave both together in the realization that in truth, they are one and the same. Miracles come in unexpected ways.

As a highly intuitive being, you must find the balance between open-hearted connection and centered strength. Don't let yourself be pulled in directions that don't "feel" right deep inside. But likewise, don't allow your ambition to create separation between you and those who are intimately woven into your journey. Horse's greatest gift comes in the balance. In the partnership of head and heart, we awaken Spirit in our action.

Horse calls for spirited adventure lead by a spontaneous connection to the energy of the moment. Trust your horse sense. Embrace your sensitivity as an ally. Harness your clear creative vision in action. Open yourself to the unfettered call of your Spirit and allow it to inspire the greater flow of you.

At one with the energy of my Spirit,
I am awake, in tune, inspired and free.

DRAGONFLY
Magic, Spontaneity, Immediacy, Change

30. DRAGONFLY

Magic, Spontaneity, Immediacy, Change

Dappled sunlight filters through a canopy of trees after rain. Diamonds of water droplets reflect from leaves and stones. From the corner of your eye you catch a tiny glimpse of light darting across the surface of a rock pool. Iridescent wings shift color in motion, hovering silently just one breath above the water, before accelerating in a different direction out of sight. The moment passes but the magic of Dragonfly remains.

A symbol of power, agility and victory to Japanese Samurai; bringer of prosperity, harmony and good fortune to the people of China; a sign of happiness and purity to Native Americans, dragonfly is an auspicious messenger of light and possibility in virtually every land it lives. To the Navajo, Dragonfly is the guide to pure water and to the lore keepers of the ancient lands, Dragonfly is the honored descendent of the Dragon.

With an ability to hover in place like a hummingbird, fly in all six directions (including backwards) and move through the air at speeds of up to 45 miles an hour (70km/h), Dragonfly is a marvel of dexterity and aerodynamic design. Born into the water realm, Dragonfly may remain in nymph aquatic form for several years before emerging onto land. Once she takes flight, Dragonfly will live only a matter of days or weeks, before mating, laying eggs and completing her magical journey.

THE MESSAGE

Dragonfly comes to you now as a great blessing, to let you know that the path you are on is sparkling with pure possibility. Dragonfly is the messenger of Light. When Dragonfly is near, so is the positive energy and spark of creativity that dreams are made of. Things may not unfold exactly as you plan, but with Dragonfly as your guide you will quickly realize that this is half the fun. Dragonfly's message is to move with clarity, but stay nimble and spontaneous. Look for the messages and shifting light on the path. Be willing to adjust your direction and adapt to the subtle call of the moment, knowing that each new twist and turn provides a new opportunity to bring, share and experience yourself in new ways. Dragonfly's message is to dance with the energy of this moment, and honor the unique light that you bring to it.

If you feel as though life's magic is enshrouded or you've lost your sense of self amidst to-do's, take time to journey to the place of the Dragonfly. Bring yourself to fresh, flowing water in a dappled forest. Come close to the sparkling surface and reflect upon the beauty of all that you see. Open to the gift of Dragonfly and return with renewed commitment to living your life to the absolute fullest. Do the simple things and the greater path will unfold without effort.

Dragonfly calls you to make each day count. Claim the gift of immortality by playing fully in the moment you are in. Be yourself in full color. It is time to claim the freedom to move through life without limits.

I dance with the light of the moment
I am blessed by the magic of life.
I move with the spontaneous call of my spirit
At one with the gift of today.

31. BEE

Creativity, Purpose, Harvest, Devotion

In ancient Egypt, when the tears of the sun god Ra landed on the desert sand they became the bees of the world. When Kamadeva, the Hindu god of love drew back his bow, the string was made of honeybees. When the ancient Essenes entered holy communion with the Angel of Creative Work, they called upon visions of bees at work, devoted to their collection of divine nectar. Rock paintings dating as far back as 15,000 years ago depict humans gathering honey from wild bees as a magical food source, as medicine, antiseptic and preservative.

When a Bee first emerges from her wax cell into the world, instantly she goes to work, first cleaning her own cell, then helping to nurse other new arrivals. She will move through various tasks and roles over the coming weeks, before entering her final role as a forager for nectar and pollen. She will travel miles each day, playing a vital role in pollinating thousands of flowers, and when she finds a spot rich with nectar, she will communicate its location with an intricate dance that indicates both distance and direction in great detail.

Beehives are a living example of highly organized, holistic and symbiotic society. Each member plays a vital role in the balance of the hive, each hive contributes life to the world around it. As essential pollinators of many of our food plants, bees remind us that no matter how advanced our technology becomes, we remain intimately entwined with the pulse of Mother Nature.

THE MESSAGE

Bee comes into your world with a clear and simple message: it is your mission to devote yourself to the harvesting and sharing of your divine gifts. Do not question it. Do not doubt it. Do not for a moment think that your gift is not needed. Do not for one second think that the absence of your expression would go unnoticed. Like the quintessential role that Bee plays in pollinating flowers to make food for our planet, you came here with a creative gift that needs to be harvested and brought forth. Your soul yearns for it. The balance of our planet relies on it.

Bee is calling you to play your part. To embark on the mission of discovering the nectar and the gold of your own being and bringing it forth to share with others. Bee says we each have our unique part to play, and while it is important to discover our own note to play, there is also deep fulfillment in dissolving into the greater chorus of the hive. Be humble and quietly focused on the task at hand. Be resilient and generous in your interaction with others. Do not be concerned if you have been recognized today for your great deeds. Allow yourself to be fed by your devotion and by the pulse of creation flowing within you (in whatever form it takes). With Bee as your guide, you will discover the sweet power of service as a gift in itself. Reward will come in the quiet witness of others benefiting from the fruit of your creation... and awakening to their own. Now is a powerful time to ask yourself, "How can my daily work and way of being serve the Earth and those around me?" Perhaps in ways that you don't even realize.

I came into this world with a divine purpose. From my first steps to my final flight, I fulfill it each day anew. I nurture myself and share my gifts, playing my part in the greater whole.

32. GOLDEN ORB SPIDER

Messenger, Balance, Awareness, Design

The sun sets in the forest. A golden silken thread drops from a tree branch, connecting to the base of a small bush. A nimble form descends down the line to a halfway point, then shoots another golden strand at an angle, connecting to the bark of a fallen tree. Positioning herself in the centre, she silently weaves a great circle around her. Intricate, balanced and strong, stretching far beyond her body, but ever connected to its source. I am Spider.

To the Native Americans, Spider is the Grandmother, the messenger and wisdom keeper. She is the Dream Catcher and the living link to both the past and the future. Spider is thought to be responsible for teaching humans how to weave. To many ancient peoples around the world, Spider plays a vital role in connecting the energy of the spirit world with that of the human world through her quiet weaving of the Web of Life.

Golden Orb Spiders get their name from the shimmering hue of their spider silk. This silk, which is made from water, is known to be tougher than Kevlar and up to five times stronger than steel. Female Orb Spiders build the world's largest webs – often over a meter in diameter – which serve as home, hunting ground, food storage and incubator of eggs. When a male Spider comes courting, he must carefully pluck the outer strings to announce himself, in order to avoid being eaten. The female will lay 100 or more eggs in the womb of the web and the male will fertilize them, before dying shortly thereafter. The female will live through the season but will pass away long before her young hatch into the world. From the moment they are born, baby Spiders will begin weaving webs of their own into the story of life.

THE MESSAGE

Dream weaver. Balance keeper. Co-creator and connector of life. When Spider visits your path, she brings valuable guidance to help you consciously design the life you truly came here to live. As Spider crafts her web to draw to her all that she needs, she comes with the reminder that you are the weaver of your own life story – more powerful and creative than you may realize. Now is the time to clear your mind and ask yourself quite simply, what do I really want to create?

Start from the centre of your being and imagine drawing together all the aspects of the life you truly wish to live. Consider the different elements of home, nourishment, creative work, family, love, friendship, prosperity... as well as your special contribution to humanity and the Earth. Choose consciously and creatively. Stretch yourself to see beyond the webs you may have woven yesterday, into a great colorful vision, knowing that as you dare to dream, this vision begins to materialize.

The more conscious you become of your interconnection to all of life, the more powerfully you will begin to draw to you all that you need – turning the visions of your dreaming into the reality of your being. Spider is your ally – consciously creative, intimately connected. Embrace your connection to the great Web of Life.

I awaken the dream weaver who sees beyond limits...
Today is a powerful day to dream.

33. GECKO

Synchronicity, Optimism, Truth, Mobility

The tribe comes together to make ready for a journey, to follow the rising sun to new lands and people. Those most worthy are chosen to row the great "wa'akaulua" (double canoe) beyond the waves into the open blue. In the ceremony of sacred fire, silence is broken by the chirp of a tiny Gecko. Warriors and elders grin in acknowledgement. The voice of good fortune has sung into the night. This journey is blessed.

Geckos are small, highly adaptable lizards found in warm climates throughout the world. They have transparent eyelids that never blink, their skin changes color to blend into their environment and their sticky toes climb walls, ceilings and any smooth surfaces with great ease. Nocturnal beings drawn to the light, they are honored by many indigenous cultures as dream keepers, shape-shifters and a sign of good luck. As the "grand totem" to the people of New Caledonia, Gecko is embraced as a great ancestral spirit to tribes of the Pacific and beyond.

In many ways Gecko is different to other lizards, but perhaps the quality that distinguishes Gecko most from the rest of the lizard family is his intricate communication and the chirping sound of his voice. To the people of Hawaii, this special call is a chime of synchronicity, affirming the high truth and spiritual significance of a moment.

THE MESSAGE

When Gecko perches in your presence, this is an auspicious moment indeed. Smile and expect good things. The best things. How would you move forward from this moment if you knew you were blessed? If you knew in your heart of hearts that whatever you committed to would triumphantly succeed? Sometimes we have unique thoughts and special ideas. Sometimes inspiration comes in the blink of an eye – as we drive down the road, walk in the trees or stand in a shower. Sometimes an idea may come that seems unrealistic or slightly beyond normal rationale, but it feels somehow exciting, expansive, inclusive. Often our thinking mind is quick to follow with questions, doubts and concerns. If we are not careful, within just a few moments a perfectly magical idea can be squashed into nothing and swept out the door.

The message of Gecko is to trust in the magic of inspired moments as doorways to future reality. Don't let critical thoughts cloud your perception of the miracles that may be ready to unfold within you now. Many of the best things in our life were created in ways that we could not have previously imagined. Similarly, much that waits to greet us on the path ahead may unfold in ways beyond our current understanding. The way to judge the validity of an impulse is not whether it seems realistic, but whether it feels good in your being. Does the idea make you smile? If the impulse stirs energy in your belly and allows you to breathe a little fuller, then hold it in your heart long enough for it to grow. It is sometimes hard to comprehend, but there really are no limits to the blessings that this life can hold for you. Within every moment, every decision, every action, every journey, there is an opportunity to choose the path of positivity and light. Gecko guides you there by simply asking, what feels most light in this moment? What feels most exciting? What makes your heart smile? Let this be a starting place for your auspicious journey.

I open myself to the magic of this moment
I listen to the call of light
I trust the inspiration that flows to me now
And follow it!

34. LOTUS BLUE BUTTERFLY

Transformation, Becoming, Lightness, Beauty

As the sun rises in the willow bog and creatures large and small begin their day, the subtle movement of a tiny wing pushes through the wall of a hanging cocoon. From egg, to larvae to chrysalis, this special being has been on a journey since the moment of her inception. All has lead to this moment, and this moment will require everything she has. But the strength she builds as she breaks free is the same she will need to carry her into flight. No other being more powerfully reflects the journey of transformation than Butterfly.

To the ancient people of Greece, Mexico, New Zealand and the Congo, Butterfly is the sacred symbol of our soul. To the Dakota people of North America, Butterfly is a living fragment of the rainbow, silently dancing the colors of Great Spirit from the sky into the fields. To other Native American tribes, while Spider's role was to weave our dreams into fruition, it was Butterfly who brought us our dreams from the heavens in the first place.

Philosopher Rudolf Steiner believed that while Butterfly was part of the insect family, her closest relationship was actually with the flower. Each of equal beauty, each equal expressions of the Divine. One destined to dance in the sky realm, one anchored softly to the Earth. As Butterfly dances toward the flower from above, flower extends itself to accept the embrace. In a moment of stillness and connection each is made complete in the other.

THE MESSAGE

When Butterfly dances into your world, she comes with gifts of light and beauty amidst the transformation of becoming all that you truly came here to be. Every journey has phases. There are times when new ideas and parts of us are first being born as seeds (or eggs!) of the possible in our world. There are times when (as larva) you begin your movement toward those visions, building the foundations of daily practice, discipline and focused intent. There are times when you must draw inward (as chrysalis) in reflection, growth and self-care. And there are times when you must use everything you have to break free from past limitations and expand your way of being... To open your wings fully, and in this life experience yourself flying.

Sometimes we can get stuck trying to solve life's challenges with old ways of thinking, when what is really being called for is a whole new way of being. Butterfly comes as a powerful reminder for you to "be" where you are on the journey, but stay open to the greater aspects of your being that are ready to come through. Whatever challenges you may face along the way are part of your transformation... Take the lesson as a gift and move on, knowing you are building the key strengths and qualities that will be needed for who you are becoming. Each step is sacred and your soul is moving ever in the direction of spreading its wings.

If the burdens feel too much to carry, remember that Butterfly moves between worlds with her lightness of being. Spontaneous and free. Awaken your connection to the simple pleasures and joys of life. Smell the flowers. Stand in the morning dew. Welcome the sunrise with a smile. Dance in the lightness of life.

I am a pure expression of God's beauty... I am light, I am free.
I have emerged from my cocoon. I am Me.

35. ORANGE BLOSSOM JELLYFISH

Transparency, Sensitivity, Surrender, Illumination

Afternoon sun penetrates the crystal waters of the mountain lake. Beams of soft white light filter down through the depths, catching the drifting motion of what appears to be a collection of peach blossom flowers in full bloom. Partially transparent and seemingly lit from within, they sway in the gentle current in a slow-motion dance of trust, freedom and surrender. I am Jellyfish.

Jellyfish have travelled the waters of our planet for over 1.5 billion years. With a balloon-like upper membrane as a body, most Jellyfish have hundreds of venomous tentacles running from their body, helping them feed and providing stability as they drift through the water. Jellyfish have no lungs, but breathe through their skin. They have no brain, but an intricate "nerve-net" that allows them to intimately 'sense' their world. Their bodies are made of 99% water. Relying completely on the currents and wind to take them where they need to go, Jellyfish are one of the only creatures in the world that have almost no ability to move on their own.

Found at all depths in all oceans (even in places where nothing else lives), some, such as the Orange Blossom Jellyfish, live their entire lives in fresh water lakes and rivers. Masters of drawing to them all of life's sustenance, these beautifully transparent beings often appear to be lit from within. When two or more Jellyfish gather together, we call this quite fittingly, a bloom.

THE MESSAGE

While many animals of the Fire realm call us into action, Jellyfish comes with an invitation to discover the sacred power of surrender. There is a master plan unfolding and the message for today is to trust the greater currents of your life. Sometimes we are so intent on fulfilling our goals and commitments that we sprint ahead with tunnel vision. Despite the subtle messages of life, we force ourselves out of the flow. Jellyfish merges the creative power of Fire with the benevolent rhythms of the water realm, calling you to be centered in your vision, but to trust completely, allowing the divine path to unfold. Jellyfish teaches us that all is provided within the flow of the tides. Action may still be required, but not forced action. Strain no more. Come into harmony with your own greater currents and surrender your agenda and intentions to the Universe. What must be achieved can be done with grace and ease.

Jellyfish reminds us not to become too rigid, but to move with fluidity and flexibility. Turn up your inner light and draw to you the ideas or energy you require. Be open to how they may arrive. Jellyfish calls us to be more transparent with others and remember that we are not alone. If you have been trying to do everything yourself, now may be the perfect time to re-organize or call upon help from others. As we empower the gifts of others to share in our journey, we open the way for greater creative expression together. When in doubt, when strained or stressed out, go to the water and float for a while. Relax into the arms of the great Mother and allow her to guide and support your way. Do less, be more and open yourself to receive.

Illuminated by the power of my inner vision
I trust the great flow of the ocean within
to guide my journey home.

36. ORANGE-BELLIED PARROT
Radiance, Expression, Communication, Acceleration

Winged one of the sun. Traveler by night. Inner knowing and devotion. Colors shining bright. Master of magic drawn from above. Bringer of secrets, expressions of love. I am Parrot.

In the Chinese art of feng shui, Parrots symbolize positive energy, good fortune and the balanced expression of the five feng shui elements – water, wood, fire, earth and metal. The Hopi people honored the 'parrot clan' of the South as a symbol of pure abundance. To other Native American tribes, Parrots – with their boisterous communication and stealth dynamic flight – were embraced as messengers of prayers, bringer of blessings to help guide the way.

The Orange-bellied Parrot is native to the Australian bird tribe and one of the only long distance migrators of its kind in the world. Traveling in pairs and small family groups, Orange-bellied Parrots journey only at night, making their way along the shores of Tasmania and across the great Bass Strait to Victoria and South Australia for the winter months. While Parrots can be masters of imitation, they each have a distinct voice and call that is their own. They mate for life and build long-term homes in the hollow trunks and branches of eucalypts.

THE MESSAGE

When Parrot flies into your world he brings a burst of fresh energy and the gift of acceleration to your path. Just as Parrot flies through the trees at great speed, angling his body to maintain acceleration while narrowly missing branches – he calls you now to trust the energy rising within and be ready to leap forward with dynamic and radiant expression. Some planning may be needed, but don't get hung up on the details. Movement creates energy and new possibility. The path will reveal itself as you take steps, and it's often easier to see what needs to be navigated once you are in motion. Like a rainbow in motion, your light will learn to bend. As part of opening the channels for your full expression, Orange-bellied Parrot calls you to communicate openly, honestly and clearly with others. Be playful and expressive. Let humor open spaces for new levels of connection. Take time to elevate your mastery of the art of listening – to others and to yourself. If you're not sure whether you understand what another has said, repeat their words back to them. Validate their expression and allow them to know that they have been heard. Ask for the same in return.

When Orange-bellied Parrot leaves the shores of its summer homeland on winter migration, it trusts the spirit of adventure and it brings all of its beauty with it. As you step out into the world, bring yourself with you in full color. This is not a time to hold back. You are only one, but your gifts are bright and many! Release the pace of the past. Take a breath. This is your time to fly!

I am an expression of God's light and color
I move with the swiftness of angels
I radiate who I am in all that I do
I am the rainbow bridge... with wings!

WOOD

"We must protect the forests for our children, grandchildren and children yet to be born. We must protect the forests for those who can't speak for themselves such as the birds, animals, fish and trees."

– Qwatsinas

37. WOOD

Growth, Connection, Support, Renewal

When Jesus needed time alone with God, the orchard was his sanctuary. While meditating under a Bodhi tree, Buddha received enlightenment. The Druids of early Britain worshipped trees as keepers of esoteric knowledge, the Greeks assigned them spirits, called dryads. Cherokee Indians honor trees as the "Standing People" and revere all plants as family and givers of life on the Earth. Aboriginal Australians honor the ancient memories held within each of their wooden instruments and vessels. In Taoist tradition, Wood brings the gifts of strength and flexibility along with warmth, generosity and cooperation.

The Tree of Life is a sacred symbol in nearly every culture. With its roots reaching down into the Earth and branches stretching up into the sky, Tree is the "axis mundi", the connective bridge between heaven, Earth and the underworld. Converting our carbon dioxide into fresh oxygen for us to breathe, trees are the lungs of the Earth. Trees bring healing medicine, shelter, homes for many animals, materials for creating and fuel for burning. Through the energy of trees, Wood teaches us much about the cycles of life, revealing the power of renewal with the possibility to bring forth fresh shoots and blossoms each spring – even when they are thousands of years old!

THE MESSAGE

When the element of Wood calls to your being, it comes with an invitation to follow the ways of the wise ones before you. As great sages and mystics have done throughout the ages, you are now being called to seek the council of trees as a doorway to the divine presence and higher purpose growing within you. Time in communion with the element of Wood is time in communion with the great circles and cycles of life. This is an invitation to your soul from the soul of the world. Accept the gift. There is new energy, new inspiration, new growth and deep wisdom ready to be shared with and through you. All you need do is say yes and answer the call.

The very best way to know what gift is waiting to unfold within you from the element of Wood is to quite simply spend time walking, sitting, playing, sleeping and dreaming among the trees. Find a special tree that calls to you. Press your hands and chest onto the trunk and feel its quiet pulse. Sit at its base or in the cradle of its branches. Let its whispered wisdom permeate your being, opening new passages of thought and vision to begin growing within.

Take time to consider the seasons of your journey. Be sure to take time to shed old layers when that time has come; to bring your energy inward in reflection when the moment calls for it; to never stop allowing new ideas and inspiration to come through; and to complete the cycle of your visions by bearing fruit to share with the world and planting seeds of new possibility in the hearts of those around you. Take time to be with trees. Share their stories, spirit and energy. Emulate their offering in your own way of being in the world – strong, flexible, supportive of others, bringer of life to the world!

I carry the wisdom of my ancestors.
I bring forth the freshness of new life.
I am the seed and the harvest.
I am balance and abundance. I am the Tree of Life.

GIANT PANDA
Innocence, Gentleness, Harmony, Balance

38. GIANT PANDA
Innocence, Gentleness, Harmony, Balance

The battleground is quiet and the armies have retreated to their trenches. Both sides are ready for the fighting to be over, but one must take the first step. From the silent mist, a special flag is raised which brings a sigh of relief. This is not surrender but a call for truce and a bold stand for the return to peace and harmony. In the center of the flag is a picture of a Panda Bear.

Chinese philosophers believe that the Universe is created in the balance of two opposing forces – Yin and Yang. With his contrasting black and white fur, gentle power and peaceful strength, Panda is a symbol for the harmony that can be achieved when Yin and Yang are in balance with each other. The rarest member of the bear family, Pandas live in bamboo forests, high in the mountains of western China, where they spend over 12 hours each day eating (mostly bamboo) in order to gain the nourishment they need to sustain a healthy life.

When baby Pandas are born they are tiny (only about 120 grams). The mother Panda cradles her cubs in her arms much like humans hold newborn babies, and she keeps them very close to her for at least the first 18 months of their lives. Besides this, Pandas enjoy their own company and spend most of their time alone, except for occasional gatherings to feed together and mate. They swim in mountain streams, embrace the winter snow and have often been seen rolling down slopes... seemingly just for fun.

THE MESSAGE

When Panda climbs into your world, he comes with a quiet but very important message. Be kind to yourself. The world around you may be racing with pressures and expectations, and it can be tempting to press yourself to keep up, but the call for this moment is to give yourself the opportunity to retreat into a space and a pace that is calming, that is soothing and is nurturing to your soul. Sometimes life calls for bursts of accelerated action, but the long-term vitality of all relationships and endeavors comes with the balance of being and doing, of stillness and action, of inward reflection and outward expression. Now is the time to measure and reclaim the balance of Yin and Yang in your life.

As a first step, make self-care and wellbeing a core value to live by. As you take time to honor and nurture yourself, you will not only find that you have much more to give others in return, you will be sending a clear message to the Universe about your choice and worthiness to experience peace and harmony amidst life's great adventure. The more you immerse yourself in activities that feel good to your being, the more those good feeling opportunities will find you and permeate all that you do. Panda's message is to open yourself to the energy of ease, grace... and genuine JOY in your daily life. Not just as a reward for hard work but as a way of being. Let go of past perceptions and programming that may have driven you to extremes. Walk the middle path and bring a sense of 'beginner's mind' to your endeavors. You will find new pockets of fulfillment in places you never imagined. As you integrate your commitment to inner harmony with the pressures of your outer world, it may be important to communicate your values with those around you and create boundaries that honor them. Panda shows us that we can be gentle and strong at the same time.

I am a beacon of harmony and peace.
I experience my life with joy, grace and ease.

TIMBER WOLF
Instinct, Guidance, Belonging, Order

39. TIMBER WOLF
Instinct, Guidance, Belonging, Order

The moon is full on the arctic plain. Restless energy stirs the night. The alpha male enters the circle watched by all. He speaks through his eyes and undertones of growl. The pace of his movement dictates the plan. By the vision he holds in his mind everyone knows what to do. He moves and they move with him in coordinated pursuit of their aim. The hunt has begun.

Wolf has roamed the earth for millions of years, feared by some, revered by many and honored as a special teacher and guide. In Egyptian Mythology, the Wolf was the scout to find the best path forward – his name meaning opener of the ways. The Tanaina people of Alaska viewed Wolves as brothers, believing they once were men. Native Americans respected and emulated Wolf's great hunting abilities because he not only provided food for himself and his pack, but also for the greater community – fox, coyote and raven – who often follow closely behind.

While often associated with the raw call of the wild, the Wolf pack way is highly ordered, cooperative and disciplined. The alpha male and alpha female are the only ones allowed to breed and normally they mate for life – ensuring that only the strongest genes are passed down to future generations. The entire pack (of 2-30 wolves) cooperates in hunting, feeding, protecting, and training the pups – with aunts and uncles often competing for the chance to babysit! While dominance may be challenged with rituals of staring, growls and body language, respect is the underlying law and fights are very rare. Many members stay with the same pack for life.

THE MESSAGE

Wolf comes to you as one of the most powerful guides on your journey to help cultivate an unbreakable line of communication with your intuition. Wolf reminds us that there is a pulse of deep inner knowing that often surpasses what the surface mind can see... He calls for a level of trust in this primal instinct that will allow you to take action when the moment calls, even when you don't know why or exactly where it is leading you. There is a greater path unfolding. Let the call inspire you into motion trusting that later you will look back and understand why!

One of the things that will help open the channels of communication with your inner guide is to bring the aspects of your everyday life into order. Sometimes we resist "cleaning house" because we feel it's not as important as the other things that need doing. But when we bring a healthy sense of focus to our schedule and order to our external world, our inner world quiets. Communication with life too becomes clearer. Wolf calls you to discover a new sense of freedom through order... while remaining open to the call of the moment!

Lastly, Wolf comes to remind you that while there are times when you must walk alone, life's truest fulfillment comes in joining energy with others toward a collective aim. Take time to honor the members of your "pack". Call them close to you and recognize each for the gift they bring. Don't be afraid to ask for guidance and help... and when the time comes, being willing to be a source of the same. When spirits are aligned, there is great power in numbers.

I am at home with my tribe
and I feel a sense of belonging in the world.
Guided by my instincts and the voice of God within.
My actions are in service of a greater whole.

ORANGUTAN
Laughter, Curiosity, Patience, Play

40. ORANGUTAN
Laughter, Curiosity, Patience, Play

Amidst the challenges that our world currently faces, there is a member of our tribe that brings a special gift that we must never forget. Found only in the tropical rain forests of Borneo and Sumatra, his home has all but been taken, but what remains in this sagely, patient and highly intelligent being is the divine gift of laughter. I am Orangutan.

With opposable thumbs and arms seven times stronger than ours (and twice as long as their legs), Orangutan is uniquely equipped to live almost all of his life in the trees. He swings branch to branch better than any other ape and much like his Gorilla cousin, serves a great role by spreading seeds through the forest – many of which can only germinate once they have passed through the digestive tract of Orangutan! Each night he builds a new nest high in the canopy – often with a roof of leaves to block the rain.

Giving birth only once every eight years, female Orangutans keep their children close for the first few years of their life. Females often stay into their teens to learn about mothering by watching their siblings being raised. Baby Orangutans are known to cry when they're hungry, whimper when they're hurt... and smile at their mothers. Armed with a cheeky sense of humor, Orangutans share the most clear expression of laughter of any animal – often in response to tickling, wrestling and playing chase. Highly observant and inquisitive, there are many stories of Orangutans escaping from zoos after watching their keepers lock and unlock doors.

THE MESSAGE

Orangutan swings into your life with a clear and simple message to bring more play into your day. Amidst the serious stakes, high pressures and apparent challenges that may at times circle your life, Orangutan brings the glorious ability to rise above tension and stress and gain a different view. A wider view from above. Upside down or from a different angle, Orangutan helps us step back, take a breath and not take life or ourselves too seriously. There is power in the perspective that climbing above can bring; in being curious instead of critical, asking questions to find a solution instead of seeking to blame; in choosing to see and expect the very best in ourselves and others, instead of the worst. Orangutan teaches us to smile (and even laugh) in the face of adversity and glide from branch to branch with grace and ease, instead of clinging to the trunk and fearing a fall, or worse. Trusting enough to play with life will awaken your inner strength and open new pathways where once a door seemed closed.

Spend time in physical play this week. Move your body. Wrestle with a friend. Climb a tree or dance with a child. Awaken the part of you that sees this life as a great game to be shared and enjoyed by all. Awaken the curiosity of the child within who sees the world as beautiful. Awaken the wise one that knows how best to coax others into play. Swing free and reclaim the power to transcend worlds. It is said that angels fly because they take themselves lightly. Orangutan welcomes you back into Earth flight through the laughter of your spirit and the divine gift of play.

My soul is bathed in laughter, my heart warmly smiles
My mind and body are at play
Life is a joyous adventure, a gift that I embrace.

41. TREE FROG

Soul song, Meditation, Creation, Rebirth

The sun has set and the rain has stopped. Birds and trees have just gone to sleep. Quietly the chorus begins. First one, then many. Each sings its own note, unified as one song with the others. They hold the rhythm, guarding the waters and dreaming our world into being.

Frogs begin their amazing journey as tiny eggs coated in jelly, stuck to a leaf over water. As the jelly loosens the eggs trickle down into the water where they will develop as tadpoles and then slowly metamorphosize into Frogs. This three-phase journey is honored by many cultures as a mirror of our own spiritual development and the path of birth and resurrection. Tree Frogs take this journey one extra step by ascending from the water realm into the dew-lit trees above. Their round, disc-shaped toes are sticky, allowing them to climb and cling to branches. Their skin changes color with the temperature to help them blend into the shifting shades of the forest.

The Celts deemed Frog as lord over the Earth realm because of its great healing powers connected to water and rain. To both Native tribes and scientists Frog is seen as a great guardian of the fresh water realm. Because Frogs live much of their life in or near the lakes, rivers and streams of their birth, they are living barometers of the health of our waterways.

THE MESSAGE

Breathe. Breathe deep and breathe again. Allow your breathing to find a steady rhythm and keep your focus there. Right there on your breath. Close your eyes and bring your attention to the center of your being. Feel the rhythm of this breathing come from this place. Return to this place. Feel your origin in this place. Feel your future in this place. All begins in the center. Drawing in your breath through your nose, allow yourself to begin to hum softly and rhythmically as you exhale. Releasing thoughts and feelings. Releasing pain and uncertainty. Humming as you breathe. Feel the rhythm building. Allow the humming to grow and allow your body to sway from side to side or forward to back. When you're ready, open your mouth and allow the humming breath to grow into another sound – whatever sound wants to come through. Stay in the rhythm. Sink into your seat. Sink into the earth. Call upon the ancestors whose feet have sung and danced in this soil. Call upon the wise ones whose faces have been painted in this mud. Whose bodies have been bathed in these waters. In the rhythmic song of your breathing, allow yourself to begin dreaming of all that you wish to birth into the world.

Frog brings you the gift of deep resonance and returning to the song of your soul. Time to awaken the sacred rhythm that calls your visions into being. There will be time for great, inspired action and that time may come very soon. But for this moment Frog invites you to sit for a time in prayer and meditation and allow the energy of your deeper Earth purpose to build up inside. Allow yourself to see yourself from way above or from the future of your path, looking back upon this moment as a turning point in your soul's journey in the world. Open to the song that is waiting within. Know that it is honored, welcomed and needed here – celebrated and joined by many. Frog calls you to sink deeply into the center of your being and allow your actions to arise naturally from the wellspring of your soul's deepest dreaming.

I am a guardian of Earth's highest dreaming
I honor this role with my soul's purest singing
I am awake and living my purpose with every breath.

42. STICK INSECT

Stillness, Awareness, Discernment, Composure

In the early days of Earth, when the elements were still finding their roles in Gaia's story, there was a time when trees were not bound to one place, but slowly they walked the land like giants, going where they were needed most to ground the energies of the heavenly realm into the Earth and the Underworld. Those days are long since gone, but there remains a small reflection of this time in the stoic life and peaceful ways of the Stick Insect.

Stick Insect, or "Walking Stick" as he is sometimes known, is a long, thin insect living in a plant disguise. Vegetarian cousin to the Mantis, colored in shades of green or brown, Stick Insect grows from a tiny egg up to 14 inches in length and has an incredible ability to pose motionless in the likeness of a twig for hours at a time to hide from predators. At times he will sway gently back and forth as if to mimic the wind and some Stick Insects have even developed extra growths that look like leaves for camouflage. The male Stick Insect has neatly folded, brightly colored wings that he sometimes flashes (while excreting a toxic odor) to ward off predators, before opening them into a gliding flight to safety. The female does not have wings so she is less capable of defending herself, but she carries a unique gift to support the survival of her species – she is able to reproduce offspring without the presence or contribution of a male.

THE MESSAGE

There are times to move with great acceleration and power. There are times to return to natural rhythms and move at a more gentle pace. The message of Stick Insect takes this spectrum one step further, calling us to return to that ancient place deep within that knows the power of pure stillness. Become observant. Open your eyes to see and take in the world with all of your senses. There is potency in silence and stillness. There is power in allowing yourself to become invisible for a time. To carry on with your own business, building up the rhythm of your work in the world without the need to be seen or noticed. Discernment is key at this time. Don't broadcast yourself or be lured by others' agendas. Keep your plans close to your heart and keep your energy sweetly focused on the simple task of nurturing the seeds you've planted and tending your garden of life.

Be patient and be grateful. The harvest time is coming. But for the moment what is brewing deep within you is simply a contract between you and your Creator. Honor it with an inner smile as an invitation to savor the sacred stillness of your being. Instead of chasing the thoughts and opinions of others, spend more time in prayer and meditation, seeking the direct counsel of your greater Source within. And from this center place, bring your expanded awareness gently back into your world. As your mind and movements slow down, your ability to see and perceive opportunity expands. You will know what action is needed and you will move with calmness and clarity. You will smile softly and those around you may not even notice as you step from quiet stillness to full fruition and the joyful harvest of your dreams.

In the stillness I am power. Nothing to hide and nothing to prove.
In the stillness I express. In the stillness I am present to the pulse
of my Creator... rising up within me.

43. RED SQUIRREL

Resourcefulness, Vigilance,
Preparation, Busy-ness

Autumn breeze brushes through the branches of an old Oak, sending a wave of leaves into drifting flight to the ground. Squirrel's tiny footsteps scurry about, collecting acorns and stashing them in crevices of bark and stone – secret hiding spots for days to come when all is still and white. Each and every nut is marked with special scent glands in the owner's mouth to be sure he will find them later. Several nuts are also eaten along the way... just for good measure. He will gain up to a quarter of his body weight as extra fat reserves leading up to winter.

In Native American lore, Squirrel is sometimes noted for his noisy chatter, aggression and gossip, but in many stories Squirrel is embraced as a great sentinel and caretaker of the forest, honored for his diligent food-gathering, for his courage in communication and for bringing loud warnings of danger to the tribe. Rising before dawn, Squirrels go about their busy-ness until after dark – pausing only for a midday rest. Sometimes they put on elaborate fake food storage scenes to fool on-looking squirrels and birds, leading them away from their actual stash of nuts. The only problem is that sometimes this must also fool the Squirrel himself for when winter comes, despite his meticulous planning, he may only find one tenth of the nuts he has hidden!

THE MESSAGE

If Squirrel has scurried into your life, now is a powerful moment to look at the qualities of your actions and preparedness in life. Sometimes in reaction to the pressures of our daily to-do's, we find ourselves running around, doing a whole bunch of activity but without real empowerment in our actions. We do ten things in a rush to get them done instead of doing the two on the list that matter most, and doing them with 100% commitment. The message of Squirrel is to pause and ask yourself what really needs to be done to make the most impact and leave yourself feeling fulfilled (not scattered and fatigued) at the end of the day. "What is one thing I can do today, that if done to the very best of my ability, will make the most difference to myself and others?" Work hard, but balance times of focus with genuine play and rejuvenation – even Squirrel takes a midday nap.

Considering the path to your great visions, it may serve you to bring attention to planning and preparing at this time, to ground yourself in the physical details of what will be required to achieve your dream. Sometimes as dreamers we avoid this vital step so as not to "box ourselves in". But the truth is that when we take simple steps to prepare, we honor the integrity of our vision and create opportunity for real freedom and peace of mind when it matters most. Squirrel also teaches us that even the best plans change and unfold in ways that we can never imagine. Sometimes the nuts we stored yesterday may not be in the same spot today, but in our search we may discover an even better stash! So come prepared, but don't be so hung up on your planning that you become rigid and unable to respond to unforeseen shifts in reality. Squirrel medicine advises not to judge too quickly or scatter your energy in chatter or critical analysis. Take a moment instead to calmly assess the situation and open yourself to perceive and receive the unexpected gifts that are certain to emerge with unforeseen changes!

With discipline and focus I build my plan...
honoring the integrity of my vision.
With humility and openness I release the "how"...
trusting the flow of Great Spirit within.

KOALA
Calm, Perspective, Imagination, Ease

44. KOALA
Calm, Perspective, Imagination, Ease

It is said that long ago, the original Aboriginal people of the Earth transformed themselves into koalas to preserve themselves when the waters of the lands went dry. These ancient koala-people transcended from their land-based Earth connection to climbing into the tree tops to drink the first rains when they returned and to chew the moisture from the leaves of eucalyptus. These wise koala-beings were memory keepers of the ancient ways and they kept watch for their ancestors' return. Some believe they are still looking out from treetops for their people to come back and to reawaken the holy wisdom and sacred ways of living at one with Mother Earth.

Koalas are not bears. They are marsupials, meaning they carry their young in a pouch. When they are born, Koalas are less than an inch (just 2cm) long, with no fur, eyes and ears still closed. The joey will stay in his mother's pouch for up to 6 months before shifting to ride on her back for another six months until he's ready to venture out on his own. He has two thumbs on each front paw to help him climb, grab and hold and he has a special scent gland in the center of his chest that he rubs against trees to mark his territory. Koalas communicate with snore-like noises and 'bellows', but they rarely have conflict with each other or anyone else. They have an exceptionally low metabolism along with under-active adrenals, so even if something is of genuine concern, Koala's response is likely to be slow and quite 'mellow'

– even in the wild.

THE MESSAGE

Moving through life at a similar pace as the great Panda, Koala brings the deep gifts of calm and ease in a unique way, for he calls us to recognize ourselves as a catalyst for awakening these qualities in others. Koala says you have a great opportunity (and responsibility) to be a source of peace and positive perspective to the world, not by preaching or forcing your opinions on others, but by simply embodying these deep values to such a degree that they radiate from your presence, positively impacting the energy fields of others. Recognize that wherever you are, you are a center of influence in the greater tribe. Your words and actions are important, but the energetic undercurrents of how you show up and 'who you are being' on a moment-to-moment basis has perhaps the greatest impact on the outcome of your endeavor and the effect you have on others. Koala says it's not so much 'what' we do (Koala does very little!!) but the energy we bring to it that matters most.

In the coming days you may have increased opportunity to bring a sense of calm, peace and new possibility into other people's worlds by genuinely embodying them in your own. Koala sleeps for up to 20 hours a day. He invites you to savor your downtime, enjoy your dreams, and consider making relaxation a way of life for a while. Koala teaches us that when we slow down enough to experience the pause between our in-breath and our out-breath, we will discover the secrets of the Universe hidden there. If others are not as quick as you think they should be to see the world through your lenses and adopt new ways of being, be patient. Love them anyway, honor them for where they are and allow each to find his own way to the well. Your first job is simply to turn on the tap from within.

I breathe deep with a warm smile
and relax into the arms of the great Tree of Life.
I feel peace, calm and new possibility.
I bring this wherever I go.

BLACK COCKATOO
Herald, Confidence,
Companionship, Communication

45. BLACK COCKATOO

Herald, Confidence, Companionship, Communication

Afternoon light stretches through the sagely limbs of a Western Australian forest. The air is dry, but a subtle shift is felt among those nesting in the hollow of a 400-year-old jarrah tree. Flight is taken, joined by others in the clan. Their great black wings stroke across the land. Their call pierces through the air announcing the coming of rain. I am Black Cockatoo.

Member of the parrot family and native to Australian forests, Black Cockatoo is honored as a sacred totem to several Aboriginal clans and family groups. Distinguished by their boisterous calls and the magnificent crest which crowns the top of their head, Cockatoos are masters of the complexities of communication – both subtle and direct! By raising their head crest with different body postures and tones of their voice, Cockatoos articulate a wide variety of messages – from defending their flock or territory to calling for their mate, expressing fear and even annoyance.

Black Cockatoos live up to 50 years in the wild and share deep bonds of affection with their partners, who they mate with for life. The male Cockatoo is known to beat a stone or stick against a hollow log in a ceremony of courtship "drumming", and can be seen feeding his partner each year while she sits on the eggs of their young in the hollows of old growth trees. Cockatoos have a unique bald spot on the top of their heads, which is thought to be a spiritual portal, giving them a direct link into the world of spirit.

THE MESSAGE

Just as Cockatoo's call comes to announce the coming of rain, he screeches into your world now to herald the coming of a downpour of positive support to grow the seeds of your dreams to fruition. When Cockatoo calls, this is a moment to celebrate. The energy of your circumstance is shifting. Go with it. Trust the greatness that is rising in you. Move with absolute confidence – as you step forward in faith, the path will rise to meet you. Expect the very best and give yourself the gift of fully receiving it. The support you need may come in the form of external assistance or an internal epiphany. It may come in the realization of an ally or rich resource that you already have access to – ready to become an even more valuable companion on your journey.

Cockatoo's message reminds us that while we each have our own path to walk, life is sweetest in partnership with others. Sometimes we become so focused on the end game of our own mission that we forget how important our relationships are and that those we love and work with have dreams of their own. From time to time, we each need validation for the part that we play. Take time to share your affection and admiration with those who are important to you. Share yourself authentically and emotionally. Don't assume that others know how much they mean to you. Take time to tell them, or better yet show them that you care. Amidst the journey of your own dreams, discover the joys of devoting your attention to encouraging and lifting up the dreams of others. Pick someone you love today and ask yourself, "How best can I encourage their journey? What is one thing I can do today to support the realization of their dream?"

I open myself to receive glorious gifts
in support of my soul's purpose.
I celebrate the opportunity to bring glorious support
to the soul journey of others.
I expect the very best...
I bring my very best to those in my world.

46. GAIA

Harmony, Abundance, Wholeness,
Forgiveness

Predawn mist settles in the hills. A hint of light stretches from the horizon. Dew rises in the grass. Leaves and branches reach subtly outward. Birds awaken into song. There is a freshness, an aliveness. A sense of celebration and awakening. Stepping into the grass, you feel these elements around you. A sense of connection with a deep pulse that rises up from beneath you, harmonizing with the rhythm of your own. Breathing it into your whole body, you open your eyes. You are home.

Ancient Greeks believed that out of the great void sprang the goddess, Gaia. The great Mother of all. Earth Mother, Mother Goddess, Mother Nature. Benevolent giver of life and Mother to all things. She was Toci, the "Mother of the Gods" in Aztec Mythology. Panchamana, the great fertility goddess to the people of the Andes. To the Hopi people she is Tuuwaqatsi – Earth Mother, honored in their first sacred law, "Land and Life are One". To the Hindu, she is Gayatri, the Mother of all creation. To the ancient Essenes, daily communion with the angels of the Earthly Mother awakened their own personal strength and infused their connection to the pulse of life around them – in the trees, the waters, the air and the earth. To Aboriginal Australians, Native Americans and virtually all ancient indigenous nations, there is a deep reverence for life and a fundamental embodiment of life as sacred – from the tallest mountain to the smallest plant or animal. There is recognition that lessons that can be learned from all things and that everything carries a purpose worthy of honor, love and respect. An awareness that as we honor the Earth and each living being on it, we honor different aspects and facets of ourselves.

What scientists have coined as the Gaia Theory, native people have known throughout the ages – our Earth is a living being, a great, sentient, self-balancing organism, constantly adjusting her environment to maintain our planet as a home suitable for life. Gaia is the inclusive energy of all animals, minerals, energy and elements. Gaia is the keeper of the eternal balance by which each plant and animal plays its part... each breathes out the air which another needs.

THE MESSAGE

As a great mother cares for her children, Gaia brings with her immeasurable love, support and celebration for your journey. She honors you for all that you are now becoming, for the dreams you are saying yes to and calling into being. She honors you for the unique and vital role you came here to play in the great creation story. Her clear and simple message is to you is YES.

There is never a time when the energy of Gaia is absent from your life or when her messages, lessons and gifts are not present and available. There are only times when you may choose to look past the signs, ignore the messages or temporarily remove yourself from your connection to the flow. Sometimes we force ourselves against the current or we struggle through the bushes in great thirst, when all along there is a river of clear flowing water running right beside (and within) us. As each drop naturally finds its way from the mountain top back to the sea, Gaia celebrates your return to the greater currents of who you really came here to be.

We can spend lifetimes living in our head, chasing ideas and concepts, external pressures and agendas, but Gaia's deep invitation is to pause for a moment and return to that innate part of yourself that truly knows why you are here. That part of you that once moved in absolute harmony with all of life. That part of you that recognizes the pulse of the Earth as our own; that honors the waters as the lifeblood of our own Mother; that hears the wisdom and stories whispered in the wind as those of your own grandparents. Gaia calls you to remember the time when you embraced the tree as your brother, when lighting a fire meant igniting the sacred embers of your own divine purpose. Now is such a time for you and your journey.

Gaia's great invitation is to recognize and embrace yourself as an honored member of the family of life – both totally unique and intricately connected to the whole. As you admire the radiance of Parrot or the spirit of Horse; as you take in the magnificence of Whale breeching or the strength of Gorilla standing his ground; as you witness the sense of purpose in a single Bee or the great vision held by brother Eagle... you not only see the beauty of Gaia, but you catch glimpses of your own being ready to be embodied and expressed. The beauty, flow, power, grace and wisdom you see in the natural world is a great reflection of qualities that you carry within. When you find yourself immersed in appreciation of some aspect of Gaia's world, ask yourself, "What do I most admire and honor about this animal/element/being?" Then ask yourself, "Where do I see this same quality emerging (or ready to emerge) in me?" Again Gaia says, now is the time.

Mother Earth is uncompromisingly protective of the balance of life, but she is also forgiving and compassionate. She never turns her back on her children. She knows that each of us is on a journey of returning to our own true nature. All of her energy is in support of this. As you spend time in communion with the animals and elements of Gaia you will find both her majesty and your own revealed in full glory. Take this moment as a gift – both miraculous and simple. An invitation to experience the most extraordinary aspects of your life as your normal way of being.

The Earthly Mother and I are One.
I am One with the energy of life.

Endangered Animal Insights

"Whatever you do unto the least of my brothers,
you do it unto me."
– Matthew 25:40

With immense gratitude and reverence for the gifts shared by each of the animals and elements in this work, I offer this short section to highlight a few of the threats and challenges they currently face in the world. The animals listed here represent just a tiny fraction of the vulnerable and endangered species across the globe. Each and every one of these creatures plays a unique and important role in the ecosystem and the greater balance of life. Just as each animal and element holds within it a special trait or quality that is needed by our world, so do you. As you are reading this page right now, my greatest invitation to you is to open yourself to the role that may be waiting to emerge within you to assist our planet at this time. Listen for the whispered call (or booming voice!) that is not willing to sit back and watch any more animals disappear from our planet. Open yourself to the impulses, ideas and visions that are ready to pour through you, propelling you into inspired action on behalf of these precious beings. Trust your inner voice. Answer the call. We each have a vital role to play. Now is the time.

ASIATIC LION
Status: Endangered
Threats: Asiatic lion currently exists as a single subpopulation,

only in the Indian state of Gujarat. It is vulnerable to extinction from poaching as well as unpredictable events, such as disease or large forest fires.

MOUNTAIN GORILLA
Status: Critically Endangered
Threats: Prize poaching, abduction for captivity, habitat loss through logging and deforestation, disease spread through humans in the forest.

SNOW LEOPARD
Status: Endangered
Threats: Poaching and habitat loss due to overgrazing of livestock. Bones, hair, claws and teeth of big cats are prized ingredients in Asian medicine. Because Tiger populations are so low (critically endangered), in recent years Snow Leopard has been targeted instead. Estimated global Snow Leopard effective population size (those likely to reproduce) is fewer than 2,500.

WOODLAND CARIBOU
Status: Critically Endangered
Woodland Caribou is one of the most critically endangered mammals in the United States and Canada, through forest fragmentation and degradation caused primarily by industrial resource extraction. Woodland Caribou have lost 50% of their historic range since 1880. With a close link to the boreal forest ecosystem, the health of Caribou populations is a direct indicator of overall forest health.

NORTHERN WHITE RHINOCEROS
Status: Critically Endangered
The white rhinoceros consists of two sub-species: The Southern

White Rhinoceros, with an estimated wild population of 17,460 (International Union for Conservation of Nature, 2008) is classified as "threatened", while the Northern White Rhinoceros is critically endangered, with only seven confirmed individuals left (including those in captivity).

AFRICAN AND ASIATIC ELEPHANT
Status: Endangered
Threatened by the loss, degradation and fragmentation of their habitat, elephant populations in some areas have declined by at least 50% over the last three generations. While elephants can live more than 60 years in their natural environment, their life span and reproduction rate is much lower in zoos.

INDIAN PYTHON
Status: Endangered
Threats: Habitat reduction due to urban development and hunting – for food and for the sale of Python skin for clothing and accessories.

TUATARA LIZARD
Status: Endangered
Tuatara, the "living fossil" (and last of its order of reptiles since dinosaurs), are endemic to New Zealand and were nearly pushed to extinction by introduced species of rats, dogs, cats and humans. They now exist only on 37 off-shore islands of New Zealand.

WATER
It is estimated that ten percent of all plastic produced every year worldwide ends up in the ocean. A UN study found that every square mile of the ocean has approximately 46,000 pieces of floating plastic in it. Plastic debris endangers our water

ecosystems and suffocates critical marine life. Toxins from plastic also find their way into our own food system through seafood that has eaten floating plastics in the ocean. We must find a way to keep our waters clean.

BLUE WHALE
Status: Endangered
Blue Whales were abundant in nearly all the oceans on Earth until the beginning of the twentieth century (numbering approximately 250,000). For over a century, they were hunted almost to extinction until protected by the International Whaling Commission in 1966. Currently there are an estimated 5,000 to 12,000 Blue Whales worldwide.

POLAR BEAR
Status: Vulnerable
For decades, large-scale hunting raised international concern for the future of the Polar Bear. Populations rebounded after controls were put into place, but currently eight of the nineteen polar bear subpopulations are thought to be in decline. Polar Bear is thought by some to be the first species to become endangered because of global warming.

MAUI'S DOLPHIN
Status: Critically Endangered
A subspecies of Hector's Dolphin found off the northwest coast of New Zealand, the Maui's Dolphin is the most endangered marine mammal subspecies, with approximately 55 Maui's Dolphins remaining.

DUGONG
Status: Vulnerable
Despite being legally protected in many countries, the main causes of population decline are hunting, habitat degradation, and fishing-related fatalities. With its long lifespan of 70 years or more, and slow rate of reproduction, the dugong is especially vulnerable to extinction.

HUCHEN SALMON
Status: Endangered
The Huchen Salmon is only found in the Danube basin in central Europe, where the remaining population is threatened by overfishing and habitat loss.

SEA TURTLE
Status: Endangered
Worldwide, six of the seven sea turtle species are classified as threatened or endangered due to human actions and lifestyles. Major contributors to the decline of their population include entanglement in commercial fishing gear, poaching and illegal trade of eggs and shells, coastal development and ocean pollution and debris (i.e. plastic). In addition to Sea Turtle, more than 40% of our planet's freshwater turtle species are also threatened with extinction, indicating threats to our freshwater sources globally.

CRAYFISH
Status: Critically Endangered
Of Australia's 140 different species of Crayfish, many are a conservation concern and 26 are critically endangered. Living mostly along the eastern Australian mainland, Crayfish are threatened by pollution, overfishing, habitat loss and extended

cycles of warm, dry climate.

GREAT WHITE SHARK
Status: Critically Endangered
Threats: Overfishing, habitat degradation and collision with shipping vessels. It's now estimated that only 3,500 Great White Sharks are in the wild, making them more endangered than tigers.

BALD EAGLE
Status: Formerly Endangered
In the 1700s, Bald Eagle population was estimated at over 100,000. Due to hunting, poaching, deforestation and widespread pesticide use, it fell drastically to under 500 nesting pairs by 1962. Bald Eagle was declared endangered in the U.S. in 1967 and its population has recovered significantly, with a current estimated population of 10,000 nesting pairs. Although no longer considered endangered, there is still significant concern for the future of the Bald Eagle.

PEREGRINE FALCON
Status: Formerly Endangered
Because of habitat loss and wide use of pesticides (especially DDT), Peregrine Falcon almost disappeared completely from the eastern half of the USA in the 1960s. The banning of DDT, combined with large-scale nest protection and release programs, has helped Peregrine Falcon recover. There are an estimated 1,650 breeding pairs in North America. In Australia, Peregrine Falcon is still listed as "rare" and "vulnerable".

WHITE PELICAN
Status: Endangered
Although it was removed from the national list of threatened species in 1987, White Pelican is still considered endangered in Alberta, Canada. Populations are on the rise (from 548 nesting pairs in 1980 to over 1,000 today) but less than half of Pelican's historic nesting islands are still in use. In North America, the brown pelican is also endangered, but populations are recovering with the support of conservation efforts.

SHORT-TAILED ALBATROSS
Status: Vulnerable
Once common, the Short-tailed Albatross was brought to the edge of extinction by the trade in feathers. Every year, tens of thousands of Albatross chicks die because of choking or poisoning from plastics and other human waste that their parents mistakenly feed to them.

CALIFORNIA CONDOR
Status: Critically Endangered
Condor numbers dramatically declined in the 20th century due to poaching, lead poisoning and habitat destruction. A conservation plan led to the capture of all 22 remaining wild condors in 1987. These surviving birds were bred and, beginning in 1991, condors have been reintroduced into the wild. Population counts in 2012 put the number of known condors at 405 – including 226 living in the wild and 179 in captivity.

PURPLE-CROWNED FAIRY-WREN
Status: Vulnerable
Threats: Loss of habitat due to farming, cattle, bush fires and weeds, plus the declining condition of creeks and river systems

of northern Australia.

MASKED OWL
Status: Endangered
Native to Tasmania and parts of mainland Australia, Masked Owl has become endangered due to habitat loss and the destruction of their nests and tree hollows. Because they only have 2-4 eggs a year, their population is small and slow to grow, but conservation efforts are helping them recover.

HAWAIIAN CROW
Status: Extinct in the Wild
The Hawaiian Crow ("Alala") is one of the most critically endangered birds in the world. As with many other Hawaiian native birds, Alala has been subject to habitat destruction from logging and agriculture, degradation of native plant life by introduced pigs, predation by introduced rats and mongoose, and diseases transmitted by introduced mosquitoes. The last two known wild individuals of this species disappeared in 2002.

WILD HORSE
Status: Critically Endangered
Two hundred years ago there two million wild horses in the United States. Due to poaching by farmers and hunters, the nationwide wild horse count is currently less than 20,000. In Mongolia, the Przewalski's horse was once driven to extinction in the wild, but has recovered with approximately 1,500 in the world, 250 of which are in the wild.

HINES EMERALD DRAGONFLY
Status: Endangered
Threats: Habitat loss due to urban development, pesticide and other contamination of the wetlands, decreased quality of ground water. Extremely rare globally, the Hine's Emerald Dragonfly is the only federally endangered dragonfly species in the United States.

BEE
Status: Endangered
Bees are in danger in many developed countries due to habitat destruction, pesticide damage, pests and disease – along with less definable factors such as electromagnetic radiation from mobile phones (which may interfere with the bees' ability to navigate) and the steady reduction in plant diversity (biodiversity is thought to play a major role in bees' immune systems. Because of Bee's essential role in the pollination of many of our food plants, their vitality as a species is very closely linked to our own.

GOLDEN ORB SPIDER
Status: Suspected to be Endangered
In October 2009, a rare species of Golden Orb Spider – the largest of the orb weaver family – was discovered in Madagascar and Africa. Because its only known habitat is within two quite endangered biodiversity locations, research suggests that these spiders are endangered.

MONITO GECKO
Status: Critically Endangered
Endemic to the island of Monito, Monito Gecko is thought to have declined due to the introduction of rats to the island and from habitat destruction caused by US Navy bombing practices

after World War II. In 1982, a survey determined the population to be approximately 18 individuals. Due to conservation efforts, these numbers have gradually increased to approximately 250 Monito Geckos now living in the wild.

LOTUS BLUE BUTTERFLY
Status: Extinct in the Wild
The Lotus Blue Butterfly has not been seen in the wild since 1994. Conservationists believe that if they still exist they may be found in only a few remote areas near Mendocino on California's north coast. Thought to have been restricted to a rare coastal bog habitat, some have suggested that climate shifts may have changed the Butterfly's habitat beyond its ability to adapt.

ORANGE BLOSSOM JELLYFISH
Status: Endangered
According to scientists, the orange blossom jellyfish has inhabited the fresh waters of Earth for 1.5 billion years. Reports suggest that this jellyfish has become extinct in many countries, but it is still present in certain parts of China. In Hawaii the presence of this jellyfish was confirmed in 1938, but in the last 15 years there have been no documented observations.

ORANGE BELLIED PARROT
Status: Critically endangered
As of 2012, the captive population of Orange Bellied Parrots was 208, with a wild population estimated by researchers in Tasmania to be 21, including just eight females. There is a target to raise the captive numbers to 350 birds by 2016/17 and to expand the captive breeding program as an "insurance" against extinction.

GIANT PANDA

Status: Endangered

Some scientists believe that the Giant Panda is a remnant species, meaning that it is becoming extinct naturally, but other research shows the Panda's decline to be directly caused by humans. Mixed reports estimate between 1,000-2,000 Giant Pandas living in the world. Scientists aim to increase the wild panda population to 5,000 by 2025.

TIMBER WOLF

Status: Endangered

Wolves have roamed the Earth for millions of years, but by the 1950's – because of encroachments on their territory by humans, hunting, trappings and poisoning – Wolves were extinct in all the states, except Minnesota. The Timber Worlf (a.k.a. Gray Wolf) has rebounded slowly in recent years and is currently listed as Endangered in all states of the US (except Minnesota, where it is listed as "Threatened").

ORANGUTAN

Status: Critically Endangered

100 years ago there were over 300,000 Orangutans in the wild. Today, both Borneo and Sumatran Orangutans are endangered, and the Sumatran Orangutan is critically so – with only approximately 6,600 currently living in the wild. Threats include poaching, habitat destruction, and the illegal pet trade. Several conservation and rehabilitation organizations are devoted to the survival of Orangutans in the wild.

SPOTTED TREE FROG

Status: Critically Endangered

The Spotted Tree Frog is a mountain stream frog from the

southeastern region of Australia. Like many international amphibians, populations have declined in recent years due to water pollution and habitat destruction. You can help protect frogs by becoming involved with water quality improvement efforts in your town and area.

LORD HOWE ISLAND STICK INSECT
Status: Critically Endangered
Once thought to be extinct, this Stick Insect is arguably the rarest insect on the planet. The only place in the world it is currently found is on the rocky island outcrops of Lord Howe Island in the Tasman Sea between Australia and New Zealand.

RED SQUIRREL
Status: Under Threat
In part because of the introduction of the Eastern Grey Squirrel from North America, the numbers of Red Squirrels in Great Britain and Ireland have dropped dramatically in recent years In fact, numbers have decreased by up to 80% in some areas due to a disease that the Gray Squirrel has passed along to it and the Red Squirrel is now endangered in the UK.

KOALA
Status: Vulnerable
Koalas are not currently listed as endangered, but there are areas of Australia (such as Western and South Australia) where they have all but vanished over time. The biggest threat to Koala's existence is habitat destruction caused by agriculture and urban development in their territory.

COCKATOO

Status: Endangered

Between the 1970s and 1990s, Carnaby's Cockatoos disappeared from much of their former range and are now extinct in many parts of the Western Australia's wheat belt. Because of agriculture practices and the loss of Cockatoo's habitat and food sources, their overall population is believed to have dropped by 50%.

Choosing Your Cause!

When I first designed this section of the book, my intention was to include a website with each of the animals to guide readers to different causes, foundations, charity organizations and positive activist groups. When I started building my list, I became positively overwhelmed by the number of people and organizations out there who are already in action on behalf of these animals and so many more. Some of the animals have many foundations and funds that support them in different countries around the world. Groups and organizations range from political activist groups to artistic movements and global meditations. What's beautiful is that each organization expresses a unique way of bringing support which is born from the dreams and visions of its founders. Wonderful and inspiring global movements have sprung from the hearts of surfers, photographers, sailors, artists, actors, farmers and entrepreneurs. Ultimately I found it difficult to choose specific organizations without feeling like I was leaving out others – particularly because these cards (and the animals they honor) may find themselves in many different countries around the world. So I decided to leave this part to you the reader, to discover and chart your own path.

If you feel inspired to take action in support of any or all of the animals in this deck (and beyond), I encourage you to consider how you might use one of your special gifts or talents to do so. Maybe you are a writer and you could offer those skills to help educate people. Maybe you're a singer and you feel inspired to write a song. Perhaps you have some finances and business knowledge that could help a charity get started. Or maybe you have a wonderful way with animals and could volunteer at a shelter or animal sanctuary. We each have special gifts to bring that are unique to us and this time is calling for all of them.

When you have a sense for the type of contribution you would love to make, allow yourself to follow where your passion leads you in terms of choosing an animal or cause to support. A simple internet search for any of the animals listed here will reveal many different approaches of support. You may find a specific organization that really matches your values and this may be a doorway to discovering a new sense of purpose, lifelong friendships and members of your "tribe". Or you may even discover as you search for which organization to support, that an idea springs into your mind for something new to bring forth that answers the call in a different way... or that takes the efforts of many and weaves them into one (my family and I did just that several years ago with the creation of a creative project called www.peaceinthewater.com)!

Follow your heart. Trust your spirit and listen to the wisdom of your own true nature calling you to play your part!

Here are just a few groups and organizations to spark your imagination and stir your visions:

World Wildlife Foundation (www.worldwildlife.org)
Animal Welfare Institute (www.awionline.org)
Wildlife Conservation Society (www.wcs.org)
Friends of Animals (www.friendsofanimals.org)
Global Animal Welfare (www.globalanimalwelfare.org)
International Fund for Animal Welfare (www.ifaw.org)
Rare Species Fund (www.rarespeciesfund.org)
Endangered Species Coalition (www.stopextinction.org)
The Cougar Fund (www.cougarfund.org)
Surfers for Cetaceans (www.s4cglobal.org)

Positive Change for Marine Life
(www.positivechangeformarinelife.org)
The Oceania Project (www.oceania.org.au)
Earth Guardians (www.earthguardians.org)

To get you started, here is a great list put together by the Endangered Species Coalition, of **"10 Easy Things You Can Do at Home to Protect Endangered Species"**:
www.stopextinction.org/10athome.html

And to take it one step further, here's a list put together by the youth of the Earth Guardians organization of **"50 Simple Tips to Help Create a Beautiful World for Yourself, Your Children, and Future Generations"**:
www.earthguardians.org/simplethings.shtml

Reading about nature is fine, but if a person walks in the woods and listens carefully, he can learn more than what is in books, for they speak with the voice of God.
– George Washington Carver

I thank you God for this most amazing day, for the leaping greenly spirits of trees, and for the blue dream of sky and for everything which is natural, which is infinite, which is yes.
– E. E. Cummings

ABOUT THE AUTHOR

An internationally published author, speaker and coach, Chip Richard's writing career spans the mediums of feature film, fiction, poetry and short stories. Chip is the author of *Writing the Story Within* (book, CD, DVD and mentorship program) and works as a creative guide with authors and projects ranging from novels and children's books to feature and documentary film. Merging a foundation of formal training with decades of creative, soulful adventure in the world, Chip carries a deep reverence for our living planet and a belief in the power of each person to play a vital role in the balance of life. In 2006 Chip, his wife and son together founded *Peace in the Water* (www.peaceinthewater.com), a global creative initiative which has brought together creative visions from over 80 countries on behalf of our planet's sacred waterways and the ancient life within them. Chip wrote *The Secret Language of Animals* and *Animal Voices* oracle card sets as a pathway for individuals and families to expand their sense of connection with the natural world and awaken to their unique gifts and higher purpose in the great creation story of life.

For more information about Chip's books and other work in the world, please visit: www.chiprichards.com.

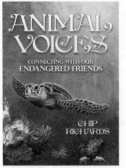

Animal Voices
Connecting with our
Endangered Friends

by Chip Richards
Illustrated by Susan Farrell

Wisdom Cards for Children

Not so long ago, the people of our world knew that all of life is connected to the heartbeat of Mother Earth. From the mighty whale to the tiny bee, every living being brings a unique and special gift. When eagle takes flight she helps us see new possibilities. When gecko calls out he reminds us to listen to our heart. When the wind changes direction or the sun comes out from the clouds, it brings a special message just for you.

Animal Voices connects kids with the unique messages from our planet's most endangered species. They are calling to all of us now. If you listen closely they will share with you their wisdom and teach you to walk in peace with all of creation.

Listen to the whispered call of *Animal Voices*... what message or gift is calling to you?

Set includes 31 wisdom cards and guidebook,
packaged in a hardcover box set.

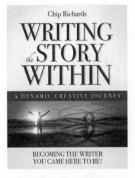

Writing the Story Within
A Dynamic Creative Journey
by Chip Richards

Writing the Story Within: an empowering writing journey to transform your ideas and experiences into magnetically engaging stories. Whether your vision is to write a novel, feature film, children's book or travel blog… *Writing the Story Within* will help you move beyond self-doubt, procrastination and judgment to fully express your true creative voice, and guide you to…

- Discover a story form used by master storytellers through the ages, from ancient Greece to modern cinema.
- Create characters with real pulses that write themselves.
- Capture descriptions and dialogue that draw readers into a heartfelt experience of your world.
- Cultivate a disciplined writing practice that frees your expression and brings you closer to your creative Source.
- Expand your connection to the stories that you both write and live.
- Express your creative visions with a structure that brings your stories to life – on the page, the screen… and beyond.

So many of us have powerful and meaningful stories to tell – tales which have the potential to weave new possibilities into the fabric of reality and truly change our world. *Writing the Story Within* offers unique insights and groundbreaking techniques to help bring those very stories onto the page.

Paperback book, 288 pages

Messenger Oracle
by Ravynne Phelan

Reconnect with the Magic of the Universe

There was a time when we 'humanity' could see and feel the Divine within each other and all around us. We were one with nature and moved in harmony with the seasons and cycles of life. We honoured and accepted the signs and messages sent by Gaia and Great Spirit. This deck is for those who yearn to re-ignite their connection with Gaia, Great Spirit, the natural world and its creatures.

Messenger Oracle strengthens our ancient bond with nature and spirit. These cards are infused with the magic of ancient dragons, elemental fae, mystical trees and their wild animal kin – they are 'the messengers' who are here to guide us back to our true nature and power and to help us reconnect with and express our inner-most truth.

50 cards and guidebook, packaged in a hardcover box set.

Animal Dreaming
by Scott Alexander King

The Symbolic and Spiritual Language of the Australian Animals

The understanding that animals can be spiritually called upon to assist us in almost every aspect of our lives is a realisation that opens a floodgate of knowledge and power to those who seek their counsel. Ancient teachings suggest that we are capable of communing with the forces of nature and speaking readily to the animals, birds, reptiles, fish and even the insects. Each animal offers its own sacred teachings. When we take the time to learn the symbolic language of the animals and listen carefully to what they have to say, we can use the knowledge gained to manifest their qualities and wisdom into our own lives.

Featuring an in-depth exploration of the Dreamtime and of Australia's seasonal wheel of the year, as well as a guide to finding your own Australian animal totem, *Animal Dreaming* explores the spiritual and symbolic interpretations of over 200 native, domesticated and introduced animals, birds, reptiles and fish in Australia. Renowned author and acclaimed Animal Psychic, Scott Alexander King presents these animals to his readers as totems, teachers, healers and spiritual allies, offering a wealth of ancient knowledge and spiritual insight into the ways of the animals. *Animal Dreaming* is an Australian first and an invaluable resource for anyone with an interest in the animal kingdom, sacred Earth Wisdom and Shamanic Lore.

Paperback book, 336 pages

For more information on this
or any Blue Angel Publishing® release,
please visit our website at:

www.blueangelonline.com